THE COLLEGE BOARD GUIDE TO
GOING TO COLLEGE WHILE WORKING

THE COLLEGE BOARD GUIDE TO

GOING TO COLLEGE WHILE WORKING

Strategies for Success

Gene R. Hawes

College Entrance Examination Board   New York, 1985

L B
23-43.3
H38
1985

V

Copies of this book may be ordered from College Board Publications, Box 886, New York, New York 10101. The price is $9.95.

Editorial inquiries concerning this book should be directed to Editorial Office, The College Board, 45 Columbus Avenue, New York, New York 10023-6917.

Library of Congress Catalog Number: 85-072883

ISBN: 0-87447-207-5

Printed in the United States of America

9 8 7 6 5 4 3 2 1

Contents

Worksheets

Foreword

Today, adult learners are close to being a majority of the college student population, as well as the most important source of growth for many colleges; however, the significant presence of mature students on college campuses is a recent phenomenon. In round figures, adults age 25 or older constituted only 30 percent of the students enrolled in college credit courses in 1972. They will constitute 45 percent of the college population by 1987, and increase to 50 percent by 1992.

Although their large numbers on campuses might suggest otherwise, adults make their way back to school in spite of difficult conditions—a testimony to their strong desire to learn. They are not supported by the infrastructure that helps high school graduates move on to college. They must seek out—often in isolation from each other—the information they need to go to college. The detailed and sometimes complicated steps involved in reentering institutions of higher education pose challenges unique to adult students.

The College Board Guide to Going to College While Working helps to make those challenges manageable by providing information tailored to adult concerns. In step-by-step detail, *Going to College While Working* takes the reader through the process of going back to school: getting information about colleges and programs; selecting the most appropriate college and program; financing education; getting admitted and going through registration; making the personal adjustments necessary to balance school and other responsibilities; and using the college's services effectively.

An adult's return to school is a highly personal decision, one which is never made lightly. Several years ago the College Board's Office of Adult Learning Services asked a nationally representative sample of almost 2,000 adult students age 25 and older why they had returned to college during the past year. An impressive 83 percent described a change in their lives as their motivation for that learning—a change that required a new competency to cope in some new life role.

Going to College While Working gives examples of such changes, which many adult learners will find similar to their own situations. A part-time waitress and mother of six found that money pressure was a powerful incentive for obtaining more education to improve her earning ability, and her children's growing independence gave her time to pursue that goal. To advance to a position that required a college education, a career fire fighter earned a bachelor's degree. A recently divorced woman with a young daughter returned to college to complete her degree in economics to assure her financial independence.

As these examples suggest, adults who seek more education are significantly different from the traditional college-age student, and have responsibilities that are at least as important as their obligations as students. Recognizing that adults may, therefore, find it difficult to reconcile their lives outside the classroom with their responsibilities in school, the author offers practical suggestions—ways to ensure that there is enough time for the 30 or more hours per week of studying that are needed for an eight to ten credit-hour program.

The very responsibilities that adults find difficult to juggle may also be their motivation for returning to school. The 1980 study, *Americans in Transition,* published by the College Board, reported that of the five major incentives for adults who cited a change in their lives as a reason for learning, the top two were career (56 percent) and family (36 percent).

Independent of their motivation is most adult students' concern about the financing of their education. Typically, adults in college have found it more difficult than their younger counterparts to locate financial resources. Federal funding for postsecondary education, the primary source of student aid, is geared toward the 18- to 24-year-old student who enrolls full-time and is supported by parents. Students who are enrolled less than half-time are ineligible for many types of aid. According to recent data developed by the Office of Adult Learning Services, roughly three out of every four adults work full-time while going to school. However, since they do not depend on parental support, such students must contribute a significantly greater share of their income to college costs than younger students who do depend on parental support. This rule applies even when independent students and dependent students have the same family income and face the same college costs.

The Office of Adult Learning Services has found, nonetheless, that motivated adult learners find ways to pay for their education. This book suggests solutions, using case histories to illustrate how adults in different financial situations, facing a range of college costs, go about putting together their financial aid package.

Once adult students are enrolled in college they may encounter additional hurdles, but there are campus services to help them. In a recent survey of urban university students, 30 percent of whom were 25 years of age or older, the College Board found that although students were generally aware of the services available, they were much less likely to use them, even when they might benefit. *Going to College While Working* offers pertinent examples of the services available and describes how to use them effectively. For example, adults who have been away from education for some time will learn that student rights are now taken very seriously, and that there are processes available to challenge grades or to deal with problems such as sexual harassment.

The College Board Guide to Going to College While Working should be one of the first books read by any adult who wants to make informed decisions about selecting a college, undertaking the work and personal adjustments necessary to study, and finishing successfully. Even motivated adult students who have clear goals for their education will benefit from the information and advice this book provides.

Carol Aslanian
Office of Adult Learning Services

Acknowledgments

The seeds of this book were sown almost a half-century ago. The author owes thanks to many contemporary pioneers in American college education. These include admissions deans and directors, and heads of programs of continuing education and other special programs designed especially for adults across the country, who generously provided essential source information.

Among them also are Carol B. Aslanian and her associates on the staff of the Office of Adult Learning Services at the College Board. They helped develop the original concept of the book and greatly assisted with detailed definition and source material. In addition, through their efforts the author benefited greatly from meetings with focus groups of adult college students enrolled in degree programs and of college educators with extensive experience in working with adult learners. These conferences were held specifically to provide first-hand information for the book.

A few years earlier, the author developed valuable background for the book through work in a College Board project, the Future Directions for a Learning Society, headed by Rexford G. Moon, Jr., Ms. Aslanian, and associates of theirs. At about the same time, further details were acquired first-hand as the author's son, Mark, continued working and raising a family while earning his bachelor's in engineering at the University of New Mexico.

Very special general understanding of colleges and college education came through work on the Board staff in the 1950s with George H. Hanford (now president of the College Board) and eminent leaders of that era in admissions and aid (including Frank Bowles and William Fels of the Board, Rixford Snyder of Stanford, B. Alden Thresher of M.I.T., Clyde Vroman of Michigan, John Monro, then of Harvard, and Eugene "Bill" Wilson of Amherst).

And before World War II, the author could start college only by studying while working, completing his first year's credits in the cooperative work-study program at Illinois Institute of Technology.

Carolyn Trager and Sue Wetzel Gardner of the College Board also have been most helpful and congenial in consulting with the author, and in very capably managing the work of getting the book successfully published.

The author is grateful to all these and still more individuals who helped. Any errors or oversights reflected in the book, however, are solely his responsibility.

G.R.H.

Chappaqua, New York
June 1985

THE COLLEGE BOARD GUIDE TO
GOING TO COLLEGE WHILE WORKING

1. Deciding to Get Your College Degree While Working

This book can provide unique help if you want to get your college degree while continuing to work at a job outside the home or at raising a family. You're far from alone in your college ambitions. Several million working men and women are actively earning bachelor's or associate degrees, according to annual enrollment surveys of the National Center for Education Statistics. For instance, more than 4 million of today's 12 million college students are over age 25. More than 5 million college students today are studying part-time.

These facts underscore three main points for you:

- More and more, working adults like you need and want a college education today.
- Colleges increasingly offer new study programs to help make a college education attainable for working adults.
- You'll have many classmates your age and older on campus. By no means will you stand out as one of the rare adults among all the youngsters.

These points suggest that it may be more important for you to get a degree than ever before. And they indicate why college can prove easier and more natural for you today than it would have been at any time in the past.

1

How This Book Can Help You

In your college quest, you can find out from this book how to:

- Get your degree by using methods that have proved practical for men and women like you who have actually earned their degrees while working.
- Plan the most effective college study program for realizing your career goals while also developing your talents and satisfying your interests.
- Identify colleges that provide the kinds of studies and other offerings that meet your needs, and choose the specific college and study program most helpful to you.
- Pay the substantial costs of getting your degree without overloading your income or credit, by using all possible sources of financial aid open to you.
- Start college with the least trouble and doubt by effectively carrying out the following steps.
  Find advisers and answers to your questions.
  Work out your initial schedule of courses and instructors.
  Handle all the unfamiliar and complex details of registration.
  Know how to approach your studies right from the start of your first class.
- Build foundations for success in your studies in the following ways.
  Make needed adjustments in your work and home life.
  Develop effective study skills.
  Learn how to manage your time to accomplish all you're attempting.
- Exercise your rights as a student if you find that a professor or an administrator is taking unfair advantage of you.
- Draw on college services, such as psychological counseling, medical treatment, child care, study skills development, career counseling, job placement on graduation, recreational sports, social functions, and cultural events.

Your Personal Guide for Navigating Successfully through College

In addition, this book is designed to serve as a handy workbook for your personal use. Whenever such aids would be helpful, checklists, schedules, charts, and record sheets are provided. These help you organize your thinking, reach your decisions, focus on your deadlines, and record your discoveries and actions. They help you keep track of the masses of detail involved in going to college.

Fill in these worksheets right in the book or, if you prefer, make and fill in copies. With these graphic devices, you can guide your progress visually. The book is designed for you to use in this and all other respects as your personal guide, reminder, and record for navigating with success to your degree.

In chapter 2 you'll be guided through actions that spell out in detail just what benefits you can expect to realize from college and what kinds of college programs can bring you those benefits. You can then decide if the benefits are important enough to justify your going ahead.

The following chapters steer you through subsequent lines of action so you can take each step in turn. Doing so will put you that much further along if the advantages of each new step prove worthwhile. But if the advantages seem too slight after any step, you can stop there. At least you'll have tried.

Chances are, though, that you'll go all the way through to your degree. Millions of other working adults find getting their degrees not only possible but rewarding in many ways.

2. Planning Based on Your Talents, Interests, and Career Goals

In almost all cases, adults in the United States turn to learning for two main reasons:

- To acquire useful knowledge and skills
- To help meet or make major changes in their lives

Those were the prime findings in one of the largest recent studies of the factors involved in today's massive upward surge in adult learning. A report on this appeared in *Americans in Transition: Life Changes as Reasons for Adult Learning*, by Carol B. Aslanian and Henry M. Brickell, published by the College Board in 1980.

Learning Needs and Life Changes

To see how these two basic reasons might work in your case, let's look at a few examples of other adults who felt impelled to get their college degrees.

Housewife-Waitress Gets into Computers

Money pressures combined with the growing independence of her school-age children stirred Jacqueline Maher to seek college to improve her earning power. She had been working as a part-time waitress in addition to looking

4

after the household with her husband and six children (ages 7 to 17). They lived in Brockton, Massachusetts.

For her study program, she went to the Massasoit Community College nearby, an inexpensive public two-year college. She concentrated her studies in data processing and computer programming. An award from the Clairol Loving Care Scholarship Program, open only to women over age 30, helped fund her studies. (Key facts on the Clairol program are given in chapter 5.) Through her computer studies she became a programmer-analyst at Brockton Hospital.

Maher said, "Having a personal identity—for example, by achieving a career goal—actively helps in marriage and motherhood too."

Fire Fighter Wins Advancement with Bachelor's Degree

As a full-time fire fighter with a home and family of his own, Harry Carter looked to college for help in moving ahead in his career. For a number of years he regularly attended Jersey City State College part-time, earning credits for his bachelor of science (B.S.) degree with a major in fire-safety management. Then he learned that he could get a bachelor of arts (B.A.) degree more quickly from Thomas A. Edison College, an external degree public college. To do so, he transferred many of his Jersey City course credits to Edison and took several tests for the remaining credits he needed for the B.A.

On getting that degree, he was promoted to a position that required a college education. He looked forward to still further advancements in the fire department after finishing his planned studies for the B.S. in fire safety.

"Not only can it be of advantage in securing employment," Carter commented on the bachelor's degree, "it can also provide a terrific lift to say that you have acquired a college degree."

Midwestern Grandmother Becomes R.N.

The arrival of the first of her six grandchildren helped spark Amy Hoch of Calumet City, Indiana, into action. With the aid of a Clairol scholarship, she entered a college nursing program that qualified her as a registered nurse. Before getting her degree, she had been working to earn extra income by selling Avon cosmetics and clerking part-time at a Sears department store.

After graduation, Hoch started work as an R.N. at St. Mary's Hospital in Hammond, Indiana. She thinks that it's up to the individual to decide whether to pursue college learning for a better career as an adult. "The decision to work or not to work is a very personal one," she said. "Some women prefer to work at home—and they do work, full-time, too."

Sons' College Plans Trigger Dad's Interest

Wartime service in the United States Army came when Herb Sandler had finished almost half the coursework needed for his bachelor's degree in accounting and marketing. When he was discharged from the army a few years later, he didn't return to college but instead started working and raising a family. Some 20 years later he helped his sons plan for and apply to college as each finished high school. He found the procedure fascinating and then closely followed their progress in college.

"When they encountered problems or decisions or exams," Sandler said, "I moved with them in spirit. In fact, I was convinced that anything their generation could do scholastically, I could do as well."

His reawakened college interests spurred him on to enroll in a college program himself—the Regents College Degrees of the University of the State of New York. Founded in 1971, this was the country's first external degree program. Largely by the part-time, independent study accepted in the program, Sandler earned an associate degree and then his bachelor of science degree.

Rest assured you will be able to work out a college program that will prove useful in the ways you need and that will help you succeed. Millions of adults have done so, using methods illustrated by the cases above. A good way to start doing it yourself is to list the advantages of a degree.

Main Advantages of Getting Your Degree

Let's start with what attracts you to college—what you'd like to gain. First, read this section through and do some thinking about it. Then list what you see now as the main advantages you want to gain by getting your college degree.

Don't worry that these benefits may reflect only your first ideas, and that you may change your mind later. Changing for good cause is fine, but it's helpful to have goals clearly in mind from the start even if you revise and refine your goals as you go along.

Noting just one or two vital advantages will be sufficient—for example, aims such as the following:

". . . to become an accountant"

". . . to realize my ambition of becoming a college graduate and to qualify as a nurse"

". . . to be promoted to an executive position at my company"

On the other hand, adults often realize several major advantages by going to college. A well-planned college education usually brings the graduate a number of benefits. To help you consider the important ones, here are the potential advantages to take into account.

Major Potential Advantages

Career and Income

Many adults put career or income goals first in planning their college programs. Their experiences have shown them that college graduates usually have better career opportunities, more interesting work, and higher pay than do men and women without degrees.

These adults often have some fairly specific career goals in mind, as the previous examples reflect. Such goals represent any one of the hundreds of different careers for which you can become qualified today through two-year or four-year college degree programs. You may already be attracted to a specific career field that naturally fits your interests and abilities.

Methods by which to develop or confirm career choices that fulfill your interests and talents are explained shortly. You'll also learn how to find out important facts about potential careers that appeal to you, as well as how to plan an education program to qualify you for your chosen career.

Skills Development

Adults often want to develop certain kinds of skills or capabilities by going to college. They may be interested in one or another highly specific skill, like computer programming, music composition, diesel-engine repair, or textile design—any of which can be learned in college degree programs today.

On the other hand, they may want to master certain broad skills, such as the ability to speak and write effectively, the ability to understand and manage people, or the ability to operate an independent business successfully.

Personal Development

The rewards of personal development attract a number of adults to college. For them, college provides the opportunity to develop their intellectual, artistic, and social abilities to the full. They also see college as important for acquiring the general knowledge of an educated person and the ability to keep well informed.

Greater Understanding

Some adults pursue college studies to gain a greater understanding of a subject or an area of unusual personal or career importance to them. They may want to develop a deeper comprehension of why people act as they do, by taking psychology courses. They may want to understand philosophies of life or religions of the world. They may want to know more about science generally, or about chemistry, biology, or mathematics specifically, perhaps mainly for career reasons. They may want to learn why the economy operates as it does, and how to manage financial affairs and invest in the economy. Or they may find it important to learn about the real workings of politics and government.

Personal Enjoyment

Still other adults find college appealing because at least some of their courses will enable them to lead richer and more enjoyable lives. Many adults are keenly interested in learning about the arts in particular—great works of literature, painting and sculpture, dance, theater, and music. While not often the most essential reason for seeking a degree, such an aim can yield an attractive secondary advantage.

Inventory of Advantages

You might pause here and, with the foregoing suggestions as background, make an inventory of the advantages you want to realize when you get your degree. Use the Advantage Inventory (Worksheet 1) to fill in your selections. It provides space for all the categories outlined in the preceding pages. Whether you choose to list a single advantage or many types of advantages, the chart will help you identify your personal reasons for working toward a degree.

You may want to make a photocopy of the worksheet for later use, in case you decide to refine or revise it. List only those advantages that are truly meaningful to you.

Planning College to Achieve Your Career and Income Goals

The following explanation assumes that like many adult students, you are informed and realistic about your career future. That is, it assumes you've already made a sound choice of career objective that fits your interests and talents. And it assumes that your career objective is realistic in terms of available jobs at attractive salary levels once you have your degree. If these assumptions do not apply to you, here are two courses of action that can help you.

1. If you have not made a career choice you know to be a really good and realistic one for you, read and work through the section of this chapter called Plan Career Goals That Fulfill Your Talents and Interests.

2. If you have decided on a career that you think is a reasonably promising one but are not sure you like (or even know about) all the important features

WORKSHEET 1. ADVANTAGE INVENTORY

1. **Career and Income Advantages**
   (For example: to qualify for a specific career; to improve qualifications for my present career; to develop career capabilities that will increase my level of income.)

   _____

   _____

   _____

2. **Skills Development Advantages**
   (For example: to develop skills in computer programming; computer servicing; bookkeeping; fashion design; public speaking; business management.)

   _____

   _____

   _____

3. **Personal Development Advantages**
   (For example: to develop greater intellectual abilities; to acquire cultural knowledge.)

   _____

   _____

   _____

4. **Advantages of Greater Understanding**
   (For example: to gain insight and knowledge in subjects such as economics, history, or science; to explore profound issues such as a personal philosophy of life, religion, or international peace.)

   _____

   _____

   _____

5. **Advantages of Personal Enjoyment**
   (For example: to expand my understanding of the arts, such as painting and sculpture, theater, music, and literature; to investigate fields of thought such as history or mathematics.)

   _____

   _____

   _____

of it, read and work through the section of this chapter entitled Checking Essential Facts on Careers That Interest You.

Now, let's apply your inventory to make college plans that will help you realize those advantages. This section tells how to do so for each type of advantage. If you didn't include certain categories, just go on to the next category on your list.

What College Programs for Which Careers

Four-year bachelor's degree programs and two-year associate degree programs are the two main divisions for you to consider. Those time designations refer to the number of academic years in which full-time students normally complete the coursework required for the degrees. Adult students who attend part-time usually take longer to complete the degree programs. Many ways by which working adults can reduce the years of part-time study needed for degrees are described in later chapters.

Some colleges offer programs leading to specialized certificates rather than to degrees. These often take less time than the two or four years of full-time study required for degree programs. For instance, high school graduates can complete courses in less than a year that qualify them for state licensing examinations, which lead to certification as real estate agents. One-year programs can also qualify persons for regular hospital nursing employment as a licensed practical nurse (L.P.N.). Better employment and career opportunities, however, are generally open to those who earn associate or bachelor's degrees.

Most often, your major source of a wide variety of associate degree programs is one of the public community colleges in your locale. Public two-year technical colleges or technical institutes for post–high school students may offer some associate degree programs as well. Four-year colleges, universities, and institutes of technology (or polytechnic institutes) are your main sources of bachelor's degree programs.

Graduate Degrees Needed for Some Careers

In one or two years of full-time study beyond the bachelor's, students earn master's degrees in various fields and professional specialties. They similarly earn doctor's degrees in three to four or more years of study past the bachelor's. These programs customarily require a bachelor's degree for entrance and lead to graduate degrees.

What are traditionally called the learned professions often require graduate degrees as a qualification or for full professional status. The following list of familiar careers includes the graduate degrees required to qualify for them and the number of academic years of full-time study beyond the bachelor's normally required to earn those degrees:

- *physician*—M.D. (Doctor of Medicine) or D.O. (Doctor of Osteopathy) degree; four years
- *dentist*—D.D.S. or D.O.S. (Doctor of Dental Surgery or Doctor of Oral Surgery) degree; four years
- *lawyer*—LL.B. (Bachelor of Laws) or J.D. (Doctor of Jurisprudence) degree; three years
- *Protestant minister*—D.D. (Doctor of Divinity) degree; four to six years
- *professor*—Ph.D. (Doctor of Philosophy) degree in the subject; three to five or more years
- *librarian*—M.L.S. (Master of Library Science) degree; two years

In addition, the M.B.A. (Master of Business Administration) degree, which usually takes two years, has become extremely popular for students interested in careers as business or government executives, though it is not actually required for employment in all management trainee programs.

Such graduate programs lie beyond the scope of this book, which concentrates on undergraduate degree programs. This book, however, can help you plan to complete studies for the bachelor's degree required for admission to the graduate program you want to pursue.

Careers for Which Associate and Bachelor's Degrees Prepare Students

Here are some of the most popular careers for which associate degree programs generally qualify students.

- airplane mechanic
- bookkeeper or junior accountant
- business administration aide and supervisor (some state licensure programs in real estate, insurance, and banking)
- computer operator, junior programmer, data entry specialist, computer service specialist
- dental hygienist, dental assistant
- draftsperson
- electronics technician
- engineering technician
- health-care technician in any one of many specialties, including
     diagnostic medical sonographer (ultrasound technician)
     emergency medical technician or E.M.T. paramedic
     medical record technician
     nuclear medical technologist
     occupational therapy assistant

physical therapy assistant
physician's assistant
radiation therapy technologist
radiologic technologist (X-ray technician)
respiratory (or inhalation) therapy technician
surgical technician
- lawyer's assistant, paralegal assistant
- nurse (R.N.)
- salesperson, marketing manager
- secretary, stenographer (legal secretary, medical secretary, medical assistant)
- surveyor
- word-processing specialist

Special Advantage of Associate Programs

For working adults in particular, one very important fact to keep in mind about an associate degree program is that it provides an inexpensive and effective way to complete the first half of the coursework required for the bachelor's degree, if planned at the outset as a transfer program leading to a bachelor's degree.

The following are popular careers for which bachelor's degree programs are required or preferred preparation:

- accountant
- advertising specialist
- architect (five-year bachelor's program)
- bank officer
- business or government executive
- computer programmer, computer systems analyst
- dietician
- editor
- engineer
- forester
- journalist, news reporter
- medical laboratory technologist
- medical record administrator
- occupational therapist
- pharmacist (five-year bachelor's program)
- physical therapist
- public relations specialist
- teacher, elementary or high school (master's degree often preferred)

These listings are by no means complete—nor should you take them as the last word for your own career preparation.

Warning: Base Your College Program for Career Preparation on Authoritative Facts

You can find reasonably reliable descriptions of the college degree programs (or other education) needed for a chosen career in up-to-date books on careers. Perhaps the most complete book of this kind is the *Occupational Outlook Handbook,* revised biannually by the United States Department of Labor and published by the United States Government Printing Office. It is available in most public, college, and school libraries. Other books you might consult are identified in the later section of this chapter called Checking Essential Facts on Careers That Interest You.

Wherever possible, base your choice of a program on the most authoritative facts you can find about its value as the preparation for a particular career. Highly significant for degree programs in a number of career areas is so-called professional accreditation. This refers to accreditation of a college's program in a specific field by a major professional society in that field.

If professional accreditation is practiced in the career you have chosen, try to find a degree program that holds such accreditation. In a number of its careeer description sections, the *Occupational Outlook Handbook* states whether degree programs in the field are professionally accredited (or approved) by an appropriate professional society. It also provides the mailing address of the professional society, for use in requesting a current list of institutions with approved or accredited programs. You should certainly write for and consult any such list in making your final selection of a program.

Central Source for Accreditation Queries

Another source of information about accreditation is the Council on Postsecondary Accreditation. You can write to the council at the address given below. Ask whether degree programs in the field are professionally accredited, and request the name and address of the accrediting association.

> Council on Postsecondary Accreditation
> American Council on Education
> One Dupont Circle
> Washington, DC 20036

If professional accreditation is not used for degree programs in the field, you might ask other highly authoritative sources about the value of one or more degree programs you're considering. Those sources of information include employers of the programs' graduates. You might inquire in a letter to one or more such potential employers if they actually do hire graduates of the programs and if they have a preference for certain programs. (You might say that you are asking in order to be able to obtain the best preparation for possible work in the career with that employer, and that the reply is only for your personal information.)

Attaining Your Income Goals through Degree Programs

The income potential of a career is certainly one of the essential considerations. The section Checking Essential Facts on Careers That Interest You, later in this chapter, tells how to find out the income range for a career you're considering. If the range falls below your income goals, you should either (1) identify and prepare for a different career with the income range you seek or (2) lower your income goals to levels that are realistic and acceptable in the light of other values and needs to be satisfied in your choice of a career.

On the other hand, if you already work in your chosen career, making degree-study plans to reach your income goals generally involves upgrading your qualifications—for example, advancement from work as a hospital aide or an orderly to the career of a registered nurse by earning a degree in nursing, or advancement from work as a bookkeeping or accounting clerk to the career of a certified public accountant by earning a bachelor's degree with a major in accounting and passing the C.P.A. examinations.

Some of the facts you will need in making such plans can be found in sources identified later in this chapter in the section called Sources for Checking Career Facts. Other sources of information are your present employer, well-informed friends who work in the field, or the offices of a trade association or professional society representing that field. Make every effort to plan the degree program that will actually lead to the stronger qualifications you seek. Just any bachelor's degree program or associate degree program is not likely to increase your income potential.

Planning a College Program to Develop Skills

Closely related to your career goals—and particularly to your income goals—are the skills you'd like to develop in your college studies. The skills that most working adults would like to acquire, or improve, through study are those useful or essential in their careers. For example:

- computer programming
- computer servicing

- bookkeeping or accounting
- fashion design
- public speaking
- business management

Students can develop hundreds of different skills in college courses, including technical, artistic, athletic, academic, administrative, and professional skills. But you may find that apprenticeships, on-the-job training, private lessons, or noncollegiate schools are more effective for certain skills areas—say, for skilled trades like carpentry or plumbing, or for advanced artistic performance in painting, acting, or music. Make sure you choose a program designed to build those skills you want to acquire.

Choosing a College That Offers the Skill-Development Studies You Seek

Two primary sources of information about a college's courses in the skills you want are an admissions counselor at the college and the college's comprehensive catalog.

Depending on what skills you choose to develop, you may take either courses needed for your major or elective courses in subjects outside your major. (Your major is the subject area in which you specialize for your degree, the field in which you concentrate much of your coursework.) Skill-building courses you take as electives may lengthen your study program, particularly if you want to take more than two or three courses in a particular skill. You need not make a decision about such coursework, however, until you do some program planning with an admissions counselor at a college.

Colleges differ substantially in the areas in which they offer skill-development courses. You may have to investigate a number of colleges to find one that offers the courses you want and also has the other features you seek. If the ideal combination of skills development and other offerings you want is not available at any college in your locale, you might have to revise your plans to make the most of those study offerings that are open to you.

How to Achieve Advantages in Personal Development, Greater Understanding, and Personal Enjoyment

For each possible advantage in the areas of personal development, greater understanding, and personal enjoyment, follow the same process as before. Find out if a prospective college offers courses that meet your corresponding needs. You can do this by examining the college's catalog or bulletin of detailed course descriptions and by talking with an admissions counselor at the college.

Colleges differ in course offerings in these areas, too. Your search for advantages in personal development, insight, and enjoyment might lead you to rule out a number of colleges. On the other hand, it might lead you to modify your thinking about some of the advantages you want to achieve in your college education.

Plan Career Goals That Fulfill Your Talents and Interests

This section guides you in making a choice of career goals that fit your talents and interests and in making a realistic, informed choice of a career. It tells how to find comprehensive, essential facts about any given career and provides guidelines for analyzing these facts in relation to your career needs and wants.

Start with Your Experience

In planning your career goals, you have an advantage over students in their teens and early twenties because you have valuable years of adult experience on which to draw. Start planning career goals that fit you, then, by using this experience. It may prove sufficient in itself for your purposes. If it doesn't, you can draw on the wide varieties of help explained later in this chapter.

Basic Career-Planning Questions

To set career goals that will really fulfill your talents and interests, you need to ask yourself two simple questions. Working out the right answers, however, may take some careful thought. Your two basic questions are:

1. What career (or careers) would I find most satisfying, based realistically on my own characteristics and those of the career field?
2. Are my choice of a career and my aims within that career genuinely workable for me?

If you have friends, relatives, or neighbors who are doing well in a career that you think you would like to get into, draw on their experience. Find out from them what abilities and interests are needed for the career and what education and training are needed to qualify. If you're already working in a field you like, find out what additional education you need to get ahead in it. Then proceed to decide on a college and an appropriate study program. But if you're not yet sure how to answer your career questions, or if you want to confirm your initial answers, the charts that follow can help you.

Check Essential Facts on Careers
That Interest You

You would be well advised to confirm all the key features of a career you're considering, even if you have information from people who work in the field. Confirming their subjective opinions in authoritative ways can give you added confidence in your decision and can protect you from making a serious mistake.

The features to check about any career you're considering include its growth prospects, its pay levels, the locales where entry jobs are available, how competitive the field is, what education, training, and personal qualities are needed, and how much potential advancement it offers.

Use Worksheets 2 and 3 to check the essential basic facts about a career you are considering. They will help you organize what you need to know about a possible career. Starting with the chart for Key Career Needs, check (or add others) what features a possible career must have to fit you and your needs. Then make several copies of Key Facts about the Career of _____. Fill in the name of a career you're considering and the basic facts about that career. Include the source of each fact. You'll find information about suggested sources in the following section.

For any career you're considering, compare your list of Key Facts in Worksheet 3 with your list of Key Career Needs in Worksheet 2. That will show you how your needs match specific career features. It will also clearly reveal any mismatches that you will have to resolve, accept, or recognize as a reason to reject that career possibility.

Sources for Checking Career Facts

A local public library, a college library, or a large high school library should have adequate sources for determining the accuracy of essential facts about almost any career you're considering. Use recent sources, for facts such as income levels and ease or difficulty of entering a given career may change substantially over a few years' time.

One of the most widely available and useful sources is the latest edition of *Occupational Outlook Handbook*, described earlier in this chapter and listed in the Bibliography. It gives up-to-date, comprehensive facts for each of several hundred careers that account for more than 95 percent of all employment in the United States.

Two related sources that you can also find in libraries may give you facts on additional career fields. Both are issued by the Bureau of Labor Statistics. The most current one is a magazine, the *Occupational Outlook Quarterly*. The

WORKSHEET 2. KEY CAREER NEEDS

1. My Abilities (check and/or fill in others)
- ☐ Good at vigorous physical activities
- ☐ Good at working with my hands, making things, running machines
- ☐ Good at figuring out technical machinery or electronics
- ☐ Good at mathematics and sciences
- ☐ Good at writing and heavy reading
- ☐ Good at talking with people, getting ideas across
- ☐ Good at managing people
- ☐ Good at drawing, design, visual arts
- ☐ Good at music performance

Others: _____

_____

_____

_____

2. My Interests
- ☐ Like work helping other people
- ☐ Like work convincing and leading other people
- ☐ Like working with practical tools, appliances, and materials
- ☐ Like work figuring out technical things in my head and on paper
- ☐ Like working in the arts—☐ design/drawing/sculpture; ☐ acting or theater; ☐ dance; ☐ music
- ☐ Like working with numbers—☐ finance; ☐ mathematics/science
- ☐ Like working with words and ideas
- ☐ Like work that's systematic and organized
- ☐ Like work that's highly independent and flexible

Others: _____

_____

_____

_____

_____

_____

WORKSHEET 2. KEY CAREER NEEDS

3. My Education Limit
- ☐ Two-year college degree program (takes longer in part-time study; leads to associate degree)
- ☐ Four-year college degree program (takes longer in part-time study; leads to bachelor's degree)
- ☐ Graduate degree (beyond the bachelor's; entry requirement in some careers, such as dentist, physician, lawyer, or professor)

4. Least Income I Need (or want)
(include at least 25 percent above your needs for taxes)
a. To start (shortly after I get my degree):
  $_____ per month
  $_____ per year
b. With experience (a few years after I get my degree):
  $_____ per month
  $_____ per year
c. Notes: _____

_____

_____

5. Competition to Enter the Career (level of competition I prefer)
- ☐ Little or no competition to enter is my preference
- ☐ Much to heavy competition to enter is acceptable to me

6. My Mobility (willingness to move to other areas for the best-paying or the only jobs in the career)
- ☐ Willing to move anywhere in the country
- ☐ Would move only if new area was appealing
- ☐ Would not want to move

7. Any Other Needs: _____

_____

_____

WORKSHEET 3. KEY FACTS ABOUT THE CAREER OF:

1. **Abilities Needed for the Career (check and/or fill in others)**

   Source: _____

   ☐ Good at vigorous physical activities
   ☐ Good at working with one's hands, making things, running machines
   ☐ Good at figuring out technical machinery or electronics
   ☐ Good at mathematics and sciences
   ☐ Good at writing and heavy reading
   ☐ Good at talking with people, getting ideas across
   ☐ Good at managing people
   ☐ Good at drawing, design, visual arts
   ☐ Good at music performance

   Others/Notes: _____

   _____

   _____

   _____

2. **Interests Needed for Satisfaction in the Career**

   Source: _____

   ☐ Interest in work helping other people
   ☐ In work convincing and leading other people
   ☐ In work with practical tools, appliances, and materials
   ☐ In work figuring out technical things in one's head and on paper
   ☐ In work in the arts—☐ design/drawing/sculpture; ☐ acting or theater; ☐ dance; ☐ music
   ☐ In work with numbers—☐ finance; ☐ mathematics/science
   ☐ In work with words and ideas
   ☐ In work that's systematic and organized
   ☐ In work that's highly independent and flexible

   Other Interests/Notes: _____

   _____

   _____

   _____

3. **Education Needed to Enter the Career**

   Source: _____

   Minimum education needed:

   ☐ Two-year college degree program (takes longer in part-time study; leads to associate degree)

WORKSHEET 3. KEY FACTS ABOUT THE CAREER OF:

☐ Four-year college degree program (takes longer in part-time study; leads to bachelor's degree)

☐ Graduate degree (beyond the bachelor's; entry requirement in some careers, such as dentist, physician, lawyer, or professor)

Other: _____

Type of major or study program: _____

Education needed for best qualifications: _____

---

4. Current Ranges of Incomes of Those in the Career

Source: _____

	Low (per year)	High (per year)
Annual income ranges—to start	$_____	$_____
—with a few years' experience	$_____	$_____
—peak incomes	$_____	$_____

5. Competition to Enter the Career

Source: _____

☐ Little or no competition

☐ Competition to enter about at average level for all careers

☐ Competition to enter is heavy (either at the point of entering training or schooling for it, or at the entry-job point)

Notes on Competition to Enter: _____

6. Mobility Needed for Employment Opportunities in the Career

Source: _____

☐ Needs willingness to move to areas that may not appeal to me

☐ Needs willingness to move to areas that do appeal to me

☐ Needs no move from my present locale

Notes: _____

7. Facts on Any Other Requirements for Entering the Career

Source: _____

Facts: _____

other, a large volume revised only every decade or so, is the *Dictionary of Occupational Titles*. It identifies almost every career in modern life—more than 15,000 occupations—and for each gives a brief description of the type of work involved. Although many other books available in libraries and in bookstores give facts about careers, be sure to consult only the most recent.

Ask librarians for help in locating such books and in searching out current career facts in newspaper and magazine articles or in pamphlet materials in the library. Articles and pamphlets sometimes provide career facts you can't find in books.

For still other sources, draw on people, organizations, news reports, and even want ads. Here are ways in which you might do so.

- To confirm what one person has told you about a career, ask similar questions of another person in the field.
- Write or telephone personnel offices of companies in your community and ask them for facts about career opportunities in their firms (tactfully requesting facts about the career field generally and not confidential information, such as specific salary scales).
- Ask for similar information at offices of the United States Employment Service or of your state's employment service, which are listed in your telephone directory.
- Read the local newspaper want ads for job openings; many include qualifications required and starting salaries offered.
- Get in touch with commercial employment agencies to inquire about qualifications and starting salaries in career fields that interest you.
- Pay particular attention to newspaper stories and TV or radio news reports about labor union contract disputes, since they often include information about job trends and earnings.

Using Books for Guidance on Setting Your Career Goals

Should you want further help in setting career goals and selecting good career possibilities, you can draw on a number of books that offer extensive guidance. Three particularly helpful ones are the following, which are listed in the Bibliography with descriptions and publication details.

A Self-Assessment and Self-Planning Manual was written by the staff of the Regents College Degrees Program of the University of the State of New York. This 104-page paperbound book might prove especially useful to you inasmuch as it was written for adults obtaining associate and bachelor's degrees without close, regular contact with counselors and professors. See the Bibliography for information on ordering.

The Self-Directed Search: A Guide to Educational and Vocational Planning, by John L. Holland, provides professional help in evaluating one's interests and using them for guidance in choosing a career.

Where Do I Go from Here with My Life?: A Very Systematic, Practical, and Effective Life/Work Planning Manual for Students, Counselors, Career Seekers, and Career Changers, by John C. Crystal and Richard Bolles, presents an extensive system for career planning and life planning as well.

Using Special Guidance Services in Setting Your Career Goals

If none of these independent approaches to planning career goals seems satisfactory, you can get help through individual or group meetings sponsored by organizations that offer career guidance services.

College Career Services

Colleges and universities that offer degree programs designed especially for adults often provide special career services for adults. These services are usually relatively inexpensive. Ask about such career services at colleges in your vicinity. To investigate appropriate career services, visit or telephone one of the following offices at a nearby college:

- Career Services Office (It may be identified by other names such as Career Placement Office, Career Planning and Placement Office, Placement Office, Career Center, Placement Bureau, Guidance and Testing Office.)
- Undergraduate Admissions Office
- Admissions Counseling Office
- General Studies Program Office
- Continuing Education School or Program Office
- Evening Courses (or Extension Courses) Office
- Summer Session Office (if you're looking for services to use between about May and September)

Ask if the college offers services like the following:

- professional counseling on career planning and career choice
- seminars, workshops, or lectures on career planning, career choice, and career information
- psychological testing for career guidance, followed by counseling sessions to help you interpret and apply the results in career planning
- services to help develop job-hunting and job-getting skills and techniques through similar counseling and workshop or instructional sessions

Tests Used in Career Guidance

Psychological tests for career guidance include the following.

1. Interests inventory tests, which appraise your pattern of basic individual interests and provide techniques for finding careers that have proved to be highly satisfying for other individuals with essentially similar underlying patterns of interests.

2. Aptitude and ability tests, which evaluate such capabilities as verbal skills in reasoning with written and spoken expression; numerical skills with mathematical and quantitative thinking; aptitude for visualizing objects or figures in three-dimensional space; manual dexterity; spelling aptitude; clerical skills aptitude for accuracy in manipulating and recalling detailed data; and musical or artistic aptitudes.

3. So-called personality tests or inventories of basic qualities of your temperament or character.

Other Sources of Career Guidance

For help in career planning, other sources available to you are local adult education programs, public libraries, voluntary organizations, and counseling psychologists in private practice.

Adult education programs offered by your local school system may provide career guidance services that include career-planning workshops, testing, and perhaps individual counseling. To find out if such services are offered, phone the adult education office (or the superintendent's office) of your community's public school system.

An increasing number of public libraries have career information centers or job information centers. These facilities typically have substantial collections of current career and career-planning information. They also often post announcements of current career-planning services offered by colleges and voluntary organizations in the community. In addition, some libraries sponsor career-planning workshops, lectures, and counseling sessions at the libraries themselves.

Voluntary nonprofit organizations also offer career guidance services. Catalyst, for example, is an organization that devotes major effort to improving career opportunities for women. It operates a career-resources library at its offices and issues publications that include a book on career planning and development titled *What to Do with the Rest of Your Life*, a manual on résumé preparation in job searching, and a series of career-information pamphlets.

Catalyst also issues a helpful reference booklet, *The Catalyst National Network of Career Resource Centers*, which lists some 200 career counselors and counseling offices affiliated with Catalyst across the country. It is available in libraries and by request to Catalyst, 14 East 60 Street, New York, NY 10022.

Other examples of voluntary organizations that provide career-planning services include the National Council of Negro Women, the National Urban League (which serves minority Americans), and the Opportunities Industrialization Center program.

An additional aid in searching for voluntary agencies and other sources of career-planning services in your locale is the current edition of the *Directory of Counseling Services*, published by the American Association for Counseling and Development. It covers colleges and counselors in private practice as well as voluntary organizations. You can find it in libraries or order it from the association at 5999 Stevenson Avenue, Alexandria, VA 22304.

Summarize the Career Goals and Other Advantages You Seek through College

Whatever approach you use to decide your career goals, fill them in as career advantages on a fresh copy of Worksheet 1, your Advantage Inventory. Fill in also the advantages you wish to realize in the college coursework you may want to take for specific skills, personal development, understanding, or cultural enjoyment.

Keep the worksheet of advantages at hand while you investigate colleges and their programs. You may want to further develop and revise your basic aims as you go along, but having your needs and purposes clearly in mind from the start can save you enormous time, trouble, and heartache. They are your essential touchstones in finding the college and program that best lead to what you want in life.

3. Finding Colleges and Degree Programs that Best Meet Your Needs

To take your next major step toward benefiting from college, explore until you find a college with a study program that provides the specific advantages you seek. Most adult college students today study part-time in evening or weekend classes at nearby colleges or at off-campus centers away from the college's main campus. It's likely that you too will choose a college close to home.

It would be possible, however, for you to choose a college hundreds or thousands of miles away from your home locale. Recent decades have seen the introduction of a number of fully accredited colleges and programs through which you can study independently and complete all work for your degree without attending any class sessions in person in some programs, or attending very few formal classes in others. This chapter guides you in exploring both kinds of colleges and programs.

How to Locate Nearby Colleges

Here are the main actions to take to find colleges within commuting distance from home or work. The steps range from simple to complex, so you may stop at the easiest one that works.

Consult Your List of Professionally Accredited College Programs

If you have obtained a list of the professionally accredited college programs in your intended career area, it will probably include the city and state of each college and perhaps the mailing address. Scan it to see if one or more of the programs are in areas convenient for you. Get the street addresses and telephone numbers from your local telephone directory if they are not given in the list.

If your list of accredited programs does not include cities and states of the colleges, you can find them in dictionaries like *The Random House College Dictionary* and *Webster's New Collegiate Dictionary* or in popular almanacs. Mailing addresses are always given in the college directories available in libraries and bookstores.

Look in the Classified Telephone Book

To locate nearby colleges, look in your local classified telephone directory, or yellow pages. If you're in a large city there may be two editions. Check the consumer rather than the business yellow pages. See the section headed Schools. It commonly includes listings for most or all colleges and universities in the general area, even including some that are a distance from the city or town.

Go through the Schools listing with care, paying particular attention to listings that include the word *college* or *university*. The list will include many noncollegiate schools of various kinds (which you may ignore) but relatively few colleges and universities. Many states do not permit noncollegiate schools to use "college" or "university" in their names. Some fully accredited collegiate institutions are identified as an "institute of technology" or a "polytechnic institute" rather than as a college or a university.

Consult the Guidance Director of a Local Public High School

If you do not live in a metropolitan area, another fairly simple way to learn the names and locations of the nearby colleges is by telephone inquiry to the guidance director at a public high school in your community. Use this approach *only* if you live in a small town or a rural area. In large cities and surrounding suburban areas the substantial number of colleges makes this approach impractical.

High school guidance counselors typically have very busy schedules, but you should be able to get the needed information if you ask for as simple an answer as possible (like the names and towns of all colleges within 50 miles).

Use the Reference Section in Your Public Library

The reference section in your local public library can be a great help when you need more detailed information about colleges. You can find directories there that give comprehensive facts about each college and cover all colleges in the country. Among the various directories are two works that are revised annually: *The College Handbook*, published by the College Board, and *Peterson's Annual Guide to Undergraduate Study*, published by Peterson's Guides.

Others, which are updated every few years, include the *Comparative Guide to American Colleges*, published by Harper & Row; *Lovejoy's College Guide*, published by Simon and Schuster; and *Barron's Profiles of American Colleges*, published by Barron's Educational Series. Be sure to use the most recent editions of the guides because programs, fees, enrollments, and many other features change often.

Consult the reference librarian about other helpful materials, which may include recent announcements by area colleges of program offerings especially for adults, in such forms as news releases, brochures, posters, or bulletin-board notices; current catalogs or bulletins of area colleges, giving extensive details on their course offerings; and information about college and career counseling services available in that library or a neighboring one.

Note Which Colleges Have Regional Accreditation

One basic fact about any college is whether or not it has regional accreditation. Such accreditation is important to you for two reasons:

1. Regional accreditation is the highest form of approval of a college or a university, attesting to its soundness and the quality of its instruction.

2. Transferring course credits from one college to another, should you want or need to, can be done far more readily if your credits were earned at a regionally accredited college. In addition, degrees from regionally accredited colleges are more readily recognized for admission to graduate schools than are degrees earned at colleges without regional accreditation. Therefore, it would be wise to consider only regionally accredited institutions.

You can find out if a college is accredited by checking one of a number of directories, among them *The College Handbook*. Another prime source of information, available in libraries, is the current edition of *Accredited Institutions of Postsecondary Education*, published by the American Council on Education for the Council on Postsecondary Accreditation (COPA).

Individual colleges usually indicate their accreditation status in their own catalogs and other literature. They typically identify the institution as a member of one of the six regional associations, listed below, which are responsible for granting regional accreditation.

- Middle States Association of Colleges and Schools
- New England Association of Schools and Colleges
- North Central Association of Colleges and Schools
- Northwest Association of Schools and Colleges
- Southern Association of Colleges and Schools
- Western Association of Schools and Colleges

Some institutions state that they are candidates for membership or are otherwise not yet regular members, meaning that their qualifications for accreditation are still being evaluated. Colleges also hold state accreditation, which is required for them to operate. Colleges have to meet higher standards to qualify for regional accreditation than they do for state accreditation.

"Full accreditation" is used in this book to mean regional accreditation for a college or professional accreditation for a study program. However, confirm what "full accreditation" means for a college or a program whenever you see it in any other publications. Some institutions claiming it have only state accreditation.

Beware of questionable agencies that may have impressive-sounding names that include the terms *college* or *university* but which function as "degree mills." Such business ventures are permitted to operate in a few states and often advertise their services by mail. They offer parchment documents claiming to be bachelor's or even doctor's degrees from the "college," for which the recipient pays a substantial price and receives little or no education. Such degrees are worthless.

Recognized Colleges Requiring Little or No Classroom Attendance

A number of colleges make it possible for you to carry out all of your study for an associate or a bachelor's degree without attendance in person. These colleges have full academic recognition for employment or admission to further study at even the most highly regarded four-year colleges or graduate schools.

Three such regionally accredited colleges have proved especially popular among adult students and have awarded degrees to more than 10,000 adults of all ages since they were founded in the early 1970s. These colleges, listed below, offer extremely flexible and relatively low-cost degree programs.

Charter Oak College (open only to residents of the New England states: Connecticut, Maine, Massachusetts, New Hampshire, Rhode Island, and Vermont), 340 Capitol Avenue, Hartford, CT 06106 (phone 203-566-7230).

Regents College Degrees Program of the University of the State of New York (open to students anywhere), Cultural Education Center, Albany, NY 12230 (phone 518-474-3703).

Thomas A. Edison College (open to students anywhere; lower fees for New Jersey residents), 101 West State Street, CN 545, Trenton, NJ 08625 (phone 609-984-1150).

Various methods enable you to earn credits for your degree from any of these colleges.

1. You can take examinations that test knowledge typically learned in college courses. To prepare for them, you study on your own using textbooks and other materials identified in special study guides furnished by the colleges. You can take an exam (or retake it without penalty) whenever you think you are ready. Some students earn their degrees entirely by examinations.

2. You can transfer degree credits earned in courses completed successfully at any regionally accredited colleges (including correspondence-study courses given by these colleges).

3. You can complete college-level courses given by a wide variety of organizations other than colleges—corporations, the armed services, labor unions, government agencies, professional societies, civic or charitable organizations. Degree credit for such coursework is awarded on the basis of credit recommendations developed by the American Council on Education and by New York State for each of many thousands of such courses.

4. You can receive special evaluation by faculty panels of prior college-level learning through various methods—for example, an oral examination in a specific subject, or an assessment of an actual performance in an art such as music or dance. Or you may be asked to submit a written report in addition to an oral or a written examination by the faculty panel.

Degree programs offered by the Regents College Degrees Program of the University of the State of New York are listed below. They are similar to the degree programs offered by Charter Oak and Edison colleges.

- Associate in Arts in liberal arts (with concentrations in any one of a number of arts or science academic subjects)
- Associate in Science in liberal arts, computer technology, electronics technology, nuclear technology, and nursing (leading to state R.N. certification)
- Associate in Applied Science in Nursing (leading to state R.N. certification)
- Bachelor of Arts in liberal arts
- Bachelor of Science in liberal arts, business, computer information systems, nuclear technology, and nursing (leading to state R.N. certification)

The Regents College Degrees in nursing are professionally accredited by the National League for Nursing (N.L.N.), and with a B.S. in business you are eligible to take the Certified Public Accountant (C.P.A.) examinations of New York State.

Although examination fees vary, earning all credits in a bachelor's degree program entirely by examinations usually costs far less than do the total tuition and fees for a typical bachelor's degree program completed in conventional courses with classroom attendance. Estimated total cost to students for a degree ranges between $500 and $2,900 in the Regents program as of 1985–86, according to program officers. Note also that some financial aid is available to students enrolled in these colleges. If you are interested in this type of program, consult the Regents College Degrees Program book previously mentioned, *A Self-Assessment and Self-Planning Manual*. It includes a question-and-answer section that will help the reader determine the suitability of this approach to a degree.

Listed below are colleges that offer reduced-attendance degree programs developed especially for adults. They charge regular tuition fees for instruction.

State University of New York Empire State College (Saratoga Springs, NY 12866); open to students who live in, or who can travel to, New York State for periodic conferences with faculty mentors at one of the college's more than 40 offices located throughout the state.

University Without Walls program at the University of Wisconsin: Green Bay (Green Bay, WI 54302); open to students who can travel to the campus every few months for conferences with faculty advisers.

Open University program of the University of Maryland (University College, University Boulevard at Adelphi Road, College Park, MD 20742); open to Maryland residents only; may involve attendance at campus sessions for several weeks a year.

Other external degree programs include the Bachelor of Liberal Studies Degree program of the University of Iowa (Iowa City, IA 52242) and the External Degree in General Studies program at Eastern Oregon State College (La Grande, OR 97850).

A national directory of such programs is the *Guide to External Degree Programs in the United States*. Compiled and published by the American Council on Education, it is available in many libraries and may be ordered from the council at One DuPont Circle, Washington, DC 20036. It describes more than 100 programs offered by regionally accredited institutions.

Be Alert to Other Special Programs and Policies for Adult Students

Search out college programs and policies that offer special advantages to you. The following are ones to look for:

- Programs that offer degree-credit courses for which you attend normal classroom sessions, but on schedules and at locations adapted to meet the needs of adult students.
- Programs that give you great flexibility not only in attendance schedules but in learning methods.
- Programs that enable you to earn your degree in less time by awarding you college credits for learning you have already acquired in your work or personal activities. (These are often referred to as "life experience credits," though that term is misleading.)

Evening Part-Time Study

Evening part-time study programs represent the oldest and most commonly offered form of programs designed to meet the needs of adult students. They make it possible for adults who work full-time at jobs or in the home during the day to attend degree-credit classes at night. To avoid shouldering too heavy a work load in outside study and homework assignments, adults studying part-time while working usually take no more than two or three courses a term for 6 to 9 semester-hour credits, thus attending class meetings for 6 to 9 hours a week. These hours of attendance by rule of thumb would entail at least 12 to 18 additional hours of study and assignments a week. The resulting week of work and study breaks down as follows:

Activity	Hours per week
Daytime work	40
Attending evening classes	6–9
Outside study and assigned homework	12–18
Total hours per week	58–67

In contrast, full-time students usually take four to six courses per semester for 12 to 18 semester-hour credits. Their study work load per week breaks down as follows:

Activity	Hours per week
Attending daytime classes	12–18
Outside study and assigned homework	24–36
Total hours per week	36–54

Don't jump to the conclusion that their fewer hours make their schedules significantly easier than those of evening adult students. To that 36 to 54 hours a week shown for full-time students, add another 10 to 20 hours a week for work at part-time jobs (which is true of many full-time students), plus another 10 to 20 hours a week for participation in skill-development labs, college sports, or extracurricular activities like the student newspaper, radio station, or drama group. Adding the time devoted to those activities by full-time students results in schedules of 56 to 94 hours a week.

Background on Degree Requirements

Earning your associate or bachelor's degree calls for completing studies that meet your college's definition of requirements for the degree. Those requirements are stated in the college's official catalog or bulletin. Almost all degree requirements are expressed in terms of credits, which are earned primarily by taking and passing instructional courses given by the college.

Academic practice generally defines credits in numbers of semester hours. One semester hour of credit represents the amount of study completed in a representative college course meeting one hour a week through a regular semester of the academic year. Thus, a three-credit course is one you would attend three hours a week—say, for an hour each on Monday, Wednesday, and Friday for a semester. A two-credit course would probably meet twice a week for one-hour class sessions.

A course load of 12 or more credits a semester is widely considered a full-time study program. A course load of fewer than 12 credits a semester is considered part-time study.

To earn a degree, you're generally required to fulfill the following:

- *Distribution requirements.* Minimum number of credits earned in each of certain broad groups of courses, such as the humanities, the social sciences, the physical or life sciences, and mathematics.
- *Level requirements.* Minimum number of credits earned in courses on such levels as introductory, intermediate, and advanced.
- *Major,* or *concentration, requirements.* Minimum number of credits earned in the subject (for example, English, chemistry, business administration) of specialization for the degree. About one-fourth of the total number of credits required for a degree must be in the student's major, or field of concentration.
- *Residence requirements.* Minimum number of credits earned in attendance at the college granting the degree (as opposed to transfer credits earned at another college).
- *Elective requirements.* Minimum number of credits earned in optional courses outside the major subject.

- *Grade requirements.* Minimum average level of course grades to be earned in all courses taken, and often in all courses taken in the major.
- *Specific subject requirements.* For example, freshman English composition, two years of physical education, two years of foreign language courses or a minimum level of proficiency in a foreign language as demonstrated on a specified examination.
- *Credit requirements.* Minimum number of credits, typically 60 to 64 for an associate degree and 120 to 130 for a bachelor's degree.

Quarter System

The foregoing credit requirements apply to general college practice in terms of semester hours. Many colleges, however, particularly in the western states, use quarter-system calendars instead of semester-system calendars. An academic year at colleges using the quarter system consists of three quarters rather than two semesters, and requirements are based on quarter-hour credits instead of semester-hour credits.

In the quarter system, one quarter hour of credit represents the amount of study completed in a course meeting one hour a week through a quarter. Therefore, credit requirements based on quarter hours generally run 50 percent higher than credits based on semester hours. For example, full-time students generally earn about 30 credits during an academic year in the semester-hour system. Full-time students on the quarter system generally earn about 45 credits an academic year, and total degree credit requirements are correspondingly higher.

Credits earned in part-time study are accounted for in exactly the same way as in full-time study. Credits awarded for learning acquired by other than class attendance—say, in independent study validated by a college-level examination—are assigned numerical values equivalent to those acquired in conventional class attendance.

An admissions counselor or academic adviser can help you select your degree program and plan your course schedule, but you should understand degree requirements well enough to take an active role in all phases of planning your college study program. Overlooking or forgetting details of degree requirements sometimes results in having to take an unexpected course and spend an extra term in school just when you think you're ready to graduate.

Weekend College Study

Weekend college programs for working adult students are provided by a number of colleges in various parts of the country. Some lead to an associate degree, others to a bachelor's. Their special advantage lies in the full schedule of courses offered during long morning and afternoon sessions on weekends and sometimes also on Friday nights. Such scheduling enables working adults to take full-time study programs (or nearly full-time programs) by devoting their weekends to classes.

A working adult can thereby earn a degree in about the same amount of time it takes a student in conventional full-time study. That is, weekend college programs enable adults to earn associate degrees in as little as two academic years and to earn bachelor's degrees in as little as four academic years.

One example is the Weekend College of the University of South Florida in Tampa (Tampa, FL 33620; phone 813-974-3218). The program offers a bachelor of arts degree with a major in either American Studies or Interdisciplinary Social Sciences. Weekend and evening courses make it possible for an adult student to pursue study full-time and earn a degree in four or five years. Also offered are a variety of majors in other fields, for which students complete three years' study in the weekend college and take the last one-fourth of their work in the major through regular class attendance on the university campus.

Courses offered at off-campus centers near the workplaces or homes of the students and courses available over local television stations are among the features of the Weekend College program. Employer tuition reimbursement programs help many students pay for their courses, and a number of companies in the area participate in the program.

Another example is at the University of Denver, which provides a Weekend College program designed especially for working women and given in Huchingson Hall of the university's Colorado Women's College Campus (Denver, CO 80220; phone 303-871-6989).

Study in the program leads to the bachelor of business administration degree. Professionally accredited by the American Assembly of Collegiate Schools of Business, the program is designed to prepare graduates for employment as managers rather than administrators. Courses are offered in four-hour blocks on Friday nights, Saturday mornings, Saturday afternoons, and Sunday mornings. Since each course is worth 4 or 5 credits, one course taken in each of any three of these four blocks every other weekend represents a total course load of 12 to 15 credits, or full-time study.

Credit by Examination

Many degree programs, including those designed especially for adults, permit students to earn a substantial number of credits by examination. Such a policy is helpful in two ways.

1. You can earn credit for knowledge acquired through life experience—

for example, extensive knowledge of a foreign language in your family background, or knowledge picked up in pursuing computer programming as a hobby.

2. You have flexibility in where and how you schedule your studies for many of the credits you need for a degree. If a moderate amount of independent study agrees with you, you can choose to earn some of your degree credits by examination.

To do so, you get the appropriate textbooks, based on the advice of your professor, program counselor, or official study guide. Then you can study the texts whenever and wherever it's convenient.

When you are confident that you know the subject, you register for and take the examination. If your test score falls below the level defined for credit, you need not have the score reported to the college. You can study further and register for another test.

Examinations Widely Recognized for Credit

The following groups of examinations are widely accepted for undergraduate degree credit:

- College-Level Examination Program (CLEP), sponsored by the College Board.
- Proficiency Examination Program (PEP), sponsored by the American College Testing Program (offered in New York State as the Regents College Examinations of the University of the State of New York).
- Examinations provided by academic departments within a college. They are sometimes called departmental challenge examinations, offered to enable students to "test out" of a course for which they have already mastered the content.

A college's catalog or counselors can give you information about the institution's credit-by-examination policies, as well as current addresses from which to obtain information about any examinations it recognizes.

Other Policies to Grant Credit for Prior Learning

A number of colleges will grant adults degree credits for college-level knowledge acquired in ways other than study in college courses—usually knowledge gained by either or both of the following methods:

1. You may earn credit for completing formal courses or instructional programs given in military service or by your employer, if those courses are among the thousands of such noncollegiate courses for which credit recommendations have been officially developed.

For more specific information, consult *The National Guide to Educational Credit for Training Programs,* published by the American Council on Education, or *A Guide to Educational Programs in Noncollegiate Organizations,* issued by the New York State Education Department.

2. You may also earn credit for your experience at work or in personal pursuits, often termed "experiential learning." A typical statement of such a policy is given in the *Indiana University Bulletin, School of Continuing Studies, General Studies Degree Program, '84/'85,* as follows:

> The General Studies Degree Program recognizes that students do gain college-level knowledge and understanding through various life experiences that are equivalent to the subject matter of specific courses in the University curriculum or that may be recognized as general elective credit. Students who believe themselves eligible for such credit are urged to accelerate their college programs by discussing their background in detail with the General Studies Degree counselor.

Indiana University's policy further provides that

- The student must be admitted and in good standing before such credit is awarded.
- Up to 15 semester hours of such "Self-Acquired Competencies (SAC) credit" may be applied to the A.G.S. degree (associate in general studies degree) and a maximum of 30 hours to the B.G.S. degree (bachelor's in general studies degree).
- After the student gets the approval of the degree program counselor and the campus SAC chairperson to apply for SAC credit, details on the procedures to follow will be given to the student.

More than 500 colleges granting credit for experiential learning are identified in *Earn College Credit for What You Know* by Susan Simosko (Washington, DC: Acropolis Books, 1984). The book also advises on how to apply for and get such credit.

Off-Campus and Branch-Campus Study

Many colleges offer courses for adults at convenient off-campus centers. Regular college faculty members teach at the centers, which are often located in office buildings or shopping malls. By cooperative arrangement with a corporation or a government agency with large numbers of interested employees, the college will sometimes conduct its course sessions for enrolled employees at their workplace. Some colleges have extensive branch campuses where large numbers of courses are regularly conducted.

You might benefit from such off-campus or branch-campus programs by saving substantial time and expense you would otherwise have to spend in commuting to the main campus for class sessions.

Cooperative Work-Study Programs

One traditional means of combining work and college-degree study is provided by the cooperative education, or work-study, programs offered by hundreds of colleges. Such a co-op program provides a way for you to gain valuable work experience in your chosen career and at the same time earn money for your college expenses.

Co-op programs are offered most often in engineering and business. The student alternates terms (semesters or quarters) of full-time employment in his or her field with terms of full-time, day-session, on-campus study. Completing a bachelor's degree program on this basis typically takes five academic years instead of the usual four.

Independent Study and Contract Learning

Some programs designed especially for adults enable students to earn some or all of their degree credits through various forms of independent study. In such programs, students confer with faculty advisers on an extensive learning activity they carry out on their own. The activity may be an ambitious research paper, a field project of community social action or scientific research documented with a thorough report, or a demanding and advanced work of art. The independent study activity must fit the student's degree program in much the same way that coursework otherwise would. The supervising professor determines the quality of the independent work and the amount of credit to be awarded. Often, independent study is open only to advanced students of high capabilities.

Contract learning is a form of independent study in which the student and the supervising faculty member periodically reach comprehensive agreements on the learning tasks the student will carry out over the next several months. Each periodic agreement is called a learning contract, and it often includes statements of credit to be awarded and grading methods to be used. Contract learning is the prime study method at some colleges—for example, the State University of New York Empire State College and the University without Walls program of a number of colleges.

Independent research projects and contract learning are also offered as options for earning some credits in a number of conventional degree programs for adults. They give you the advantages of flexibility and the opportunity to learn on your own initiative. If those factors appeal to you, find out from the college's catalog or admissions office if they are features of its adult program.

Correspondence Courses

Many degree programs for adult students permit you to earn at least some credits toward your degree through correspondence courses offered by regionally accredited colleges and universities. Hundreds of such courses are available. They offer the advantage of flexibility in schedule and location. This form of independent study is highly structured, with specific lesson assignments and the availability of professorial advice by letter or phone. Some colleges have toll-free numbers for long-distance calls.

Again, a college's literature or advisers can tell you if it accepts correspondence-course study for credits in a degree program you're considering. To get an idea of the wide range of correspondence courses from which you might choose, consult the current edition of *The Independent Study Catalog*, compiled by the National University Continuing Education Association (NUCEA), which can be found in many libraries and bookstores.

Tuition fees for college-credit correspondence courses are generally about the same as tuition charges for attending similar courses at the college. But taking correspondence courses eliminates the expense of traveling to and from classes.

Unique Degree Programs Designed by Individual Colleges

Unusual advantages are available through some of the many unique degree-credit programs especially designed for adult students by individual colleges. Be aggressive in looking for information about such offerings in sources like local news accounts and announcements and bulletins sent to libraries. Scrutinize and analyze college literature minutely and critically for special programs that may be of particular help to you. Here are a couple of examples of such offerings.

Fordham University's EXCEL Program

Through the EXCEL program of Fordham University in New York City, an adult who is holding a full-time job can earn a bachelor's degree in the four-year period customary for full-time students. EXCEL is an introductory program meeting Fordham's core-curriculum (distribution) requirements for the bachelor's degree. The program offers five specially developed interdisciplinary courses in the humanities and social sciences worth 6 credits each, and five special introductory courses in the physical and life sciences and mathematics worth 4 credits each. Students are required to complete four courses from each of the two groups for a total of 40 credits.

The program offers a wide variety of scheduling options: courses are given weekday mornings, afternoons, and evenings and on Saturdays. Some courses are even offered at varying times through the week to accommodate the needs of persons working similarly varying or swing-shift hours. EXCEL classes commonly meet for three-hour sessions one day a week with an additional session on Saturday once a month.

Able students with no previous college experience usually complete their required 40-credit EXCEL studies in a little over a year, taking maximum credits as follows:

Fall semester	12 credits
January interterm	4 credits
Spring semester	12 credits
Summer session	6 or 8 credits
Total credits per year	34 to 36 credits

EXCEL credits lead to subsequent completion of studies for the Fordham bachelor of arts degree, which requires a total of at least 128 credits. The 88 further degree credits beyond the 40 earned in EXCEL may be earned as follows:

32 credits in a major (minimum required; majors in subjects including computer science can be completed in Fordham evening courses)
40 credits (maximum) through life-experience evaluation
16 credits in elective courses (or in preprofessional courses in preparation for graduate study)

Able students working full-time can go on to complete these credit requirements at Fordham within four years of entering EXCEL. Fordham offers all this coursework at its Lincoln Center campus in New York City.

Off-Campus Bachelor's Programs of the University of Redlands

For persons who have associate degrees or have otherwise completed the first two years of full-time college study, the University of Redlands in Redlands, California, offers courses for a bachelor's degree in business and management and for a bachelor of science degree in health science at many off-campus locations throughout southern California. A number of these are the sites of businesses, hospitals, and industrial corporations—among them GTE in Santa Monica, General Dynamics in San Diego, Hughes Aircraft in

El Segundo, Jet Propulsion Laboratory in Pasadena, Medical Center of Garden Grove, and Textron in Santa Ana.

Designed for adult students working full-time, the two bachelor's degree programs have special core-curriculum sequences in class sessions that meet for four hours one evening a week year-round.

By attending one night a week, a student can usually complete 32 or more core credits in 12 to 16 months. Up to 40 additional credits may be earned by the evaluation of prior learning and experience described in a Life-Learning Portfolio prepared by all students as part of the program. Completing all the requirements for a bachelor's degree takes many students no more than the two years normally required past the associate degree to earn the bachelor's in full-time study.

The following list provides a convenient summary of the college degree programs designed especially for adults. For each program or policy it lists major potential advantages and thus serves as a checklist in your evaluation of degree-credit programs.

Summary of Special Adult Programs and Policies with Their Advantages

Program or Policy	*Major Advantages*
1. Evening part-time study	Enables adults who work full-time to earn degrees entirely by part-time study.
2. Weekend college study	Enables adults who work full-time to earn degrees by attending weekend classes. Total time is about the same as in conventional full-time study.
3. Credit by examination	Enables students to earn substantial credit through tests evaluating prior learning or independent study.
4. Credit for experiential learning	Enables students to save time and tuition costs by earning credit for prior learning.

5. Off-campus and branch-
   campus study

Enables students to save time and
expense of extra travel sometimes
required to attend classes.

6. Cooperative work-study

Enables students to gain valuable
career experience and to earn large
part of college costs.

7. Independent study and
   contract learning

Enables students to earn substantial
credit through flexible independent
study.

8. Correspondence coursework

Permits flexible independent study
but provides more structure and
teacher guidance than in completely
independent study programs.

9. Unique degree programs
   designed by individual colleges

Coursework and schedules tailored to
the special needs of working adult
students.

Get Ready to Gather More Detailed Information

Once you've completed your basic investigations, assemble the names, addresses, and telephone numbers of colleges from which to request detailed
information. Also, start jotting down pertinent facts about each college that
interests you—facts about its programs, services, requirements, and any
special features.

Among the colleges to contact are those within convenient commuting
distance and those that require little or no classroom attendance (particularly
if no nearby college seems to meet your needs). Organize your records and
notes for each college on separate sheets and keep them in file folders or
large envelopes, because you'll soon have a mass of booklets, folders, brochures, letters, and forms to keep track of.

To request college and program information, use the same basic format
each time you ask for informational materials from a college. For your
convenience a suggested form letter for requests made by mail is given
below. This is followed by sample questions and comments to use when you
request information by phone.

Suggested Form Letter for Requesting Information

(your mailing address)
(date)

Admissions Director
(Name of Program or Division, if you have it)
(College Name)
(College mailing address)

Dear Sir or Madam:
Please send me your catalog and other informational materials for prospective adult students who wish to consider studying for an associate or a bachelor's degree. I am especially interested in receiving material on special programs and services you offer for adult students.

Will you please also send forms and information needed in applying for admission and for financial aid.

Thank you for your help.

Sincerely yours,
(signature)
(your name, typed or printed)

Suggested Questions and Comments for Phone Requests

Telephone the main switchboard of the college or, if you have it, dial the phone number of the undergraduate admissions office or the office of the special adult study program that interests you. If you phone the main switchboard:
"I'd like the Office of Undergraduate Admissions, please."
After you are connected with the admissions office or the office of the special adult study program:
"May I speak to an admissions counselor or another adviser who can give me information about your programs for adult students?"
Wait for another person to take your call or for the person who answered to say he or she can help you.
"My name is _____ _____. I'm an adult, and I cannot go to college on a regular full-time basis during the day or on weekdays. But I would like to earn my associate [bachelor's] degree from your college. Would that be possible for me to do?"
Listen to the person's answer and respond as appropriate. If the answer is basically yes, continue as follows.
"Could you send me a catalog and other informational materials explaining how I can earn my degree at your college? I'm especially interested in

receiving material on any special programs and services you offer for adult students. And I'd appreciate it if you could also send copies of the application forms and all the information I'd need to apply for admission and for financial aid."

Before the conversation ends, it's wise to verify information.

"Let me spell my name and give you my mailing address, with my zip code."

Give your name and give and confirm your mailing address.

"Thank you very much for your help. Would you please tell me your name again? Would you spell that for me, please? And if I have any further questions, may I phone you at this number?"

Give the number. If the answer is no, take down the name and phone number of the person who will help you. Repeat your thanks.

Follow-Up Requests

Keep copies of the letters you send and keep a record of the dates of your phone inquiries. If, through some oversight, the information you've requested doesn't arrive in about two weeks, you'll have details at hand to make a follow-up inquiry.

Examine all the material you receive. Be alert to even passing mention of any programs, services, policies, or provisions that might be interesting or helpful to you. These could include special review and refresher sessions for adults resuming studies after a number of years, study skills development centers, workshops for college orientation or for career and study planning, and on-campus child-care services.

Make follow-up requests for details on any potentially useful programs or services mentioned in the college literature you receive. Doing so might uncover valuable information.

Colleges usually send modest literature like printed brochures or booklets and typewritten bulletins for specific programs at no charge to prospective students. They rarely send free copies of their complete catalogs, which are printed paperbound books up to several hundred pages long. If you want a complete catalog, you may have to pay several dollars, and at this point in your investigations you probably don't need the highly detailed information it provides.

4. Choosing the Most Advantageous College and Program

You will want to choose a college with a program that offers you the most benefits. Here are the main steps to take in the vital process of making your choice.

1. Systematically screen the college literature you receive to identify the better possibilities. Make all necessary requests for follow-up details and for data on still other programs you may learn of.

2. Thoroughly investigate your better possibilities: visit each college you might want to attend and talk to the persons who can give you useful information. Analyze the information you get and probe hard for more if you think you need it.

3. When you're ready to make a final choice, compare all factors to determine your best options.

Screen College Information on the Basis of Your Needs and Other Key Factors

Use Worksheet 4 to help you make an initial evaluation of the various colleges that have sent information to you. Make several photocopies of the worksheet—one for each college you are considering.

First, look through the college's literature with your filled-in Advantage

Inventory (Worksheet 1 in chapter 2) at hand. Now you can begin to see whether a college's offerings will help you gain the advantages you want in getting a degree.

Career advantages will probably take priority. Does a major or concentration in a degree program that you are considering provide the qualifications needed to enter the career field you've picked as your goal? Check the appropriate box on the Worksheet 4 form for this college and jot down any important notes. For example, if the answer is "no," but the college offers preparation for a closely related career field, it will be useful to note that information. Or you could write down alternative careers for which preparation is available—other career fields that may fit your interests and abilities although they are not your first choice.

Continuing down the worksheet, search in the college and study program materials for information about professional accreditation of the study programs the college offers in your career field. If you have a list of currently accredited programs in the career field (see chapter 2), use it to cross-check such professional accreditation.

It will be helpful as well to use the college information to verify whether your degree objective in career-preparation studies should be an associate or a bachelor's degree, and to note other possible advantages or drawbacks of the college's offerings for your career studies. These might be such factors as the availability of special work experience or internships in the study program, the high job placement of graduates, or an introduction to the latest advances in the field.

Analyze All Your Associate Degree Options

You may have valuable options that should not be overlooked in the range of associate degree programs typically offered by two-year community colleges. If you have not already done so, request information from such colleges in your vicinity, regardless of your career aims. You might similarly request information from any public two-year technical colleges or vocational/technical institutes in your area.

Community college programs can be helpful for three main reasons.

1. Community colleges typically offer preparatory programs in careers with job openings in the area, and in wide varieties of fields.

2. These colleges also offer sound study programs covering the first half of four-year bachelor's degree programs at convenient locations and at low cost; such study programs are called transfer programs.

Programs designed primarily to prepare graduates for employment rather than further study for the bachelor's after receipt of the associate degree are

WORKSHEET 4. EVALUATION OF A COLLEGE'S INFORMATION

Name of College: ⎯⎯⎯⎯⎯⎯⎯⎯⎯⎯⎯⎯⎯⎯⎯⎯⎯⎯⎯⎯⎯⎯⎯⎯⎯

Program (or Degree or School): ⎯⎯⎯⎯⎯⎯⎯⎯⎯⎯⎯⎯⎯⎯⎯⎯⎯

My Needs—How Well Does It Meet Them?

1. **My career aims**
   a. Does this college/program provide studies that qualify me for my intended career field? ☐ Yes ☐ No
   Notes (closest studies it does offer, alternatives it offers, etc.):

   ⎯⎯⎯⎯⎯⎯⎯⎯⎯⎯⎯⎯⎯⎯⎯⎯⎯⎯⎯⎯⎯⎯⎯⎯⎯⎯⎯⎯⎯⎯⎯⎯

   ⎯⎯⎯⎯⎯⎯⎯⎯⎯⎯⎯⎯⎯⎯⎯⎯⎯⎯⎯⎯⎯⎯⎯⎯⎯⎯⎯⎯⎯⎯⎯⎯

   ⎯⎯⎯⎯⎯⎯⎯⎯⎯⎯⎯⎯⎯⎯⎯⎯⎯⎯⎯⎯⎯⎯⎯⎯⎯⎯⎯⎯⎯⎯⎯⎯

   ⎯⎯⎯⎯⎯⎯⎯⎯⎯⎯⎯⎯⎯⎯⎯⎯⎯⎯⎯⎯⎯⎯⎯⎯⎯⎯⎯⎯⎯⎯⎯⎯

   b. If "yes" to a, is its study program professionally accredited?
   ☐ Yes ☐ No ☐ Professional accreditation not used in this field. Notes:

   ⎯⎯⎯⎯⎯⎯⎯⎯⎯⎯⎯⎯⎯⎯⎯⎯⎯⎯⎯⎯⎯⎯⎯⎯⎯⎯⎯⎯⎯⎯⎯⎯

   ⎯⎯⎯⎯⎯⎯⎯⎯⎯⎯⎯⎯⎯⎯⎯⎯⎯⎯⎯⎯⎯⎯⎯⎯⎯⎯⎯⎯⎯⎯⎯⎯

   ⎯⎯⎯⎯⎯⎯⎯⎯⎯⎯⎯⎯⎯⎯⎯⎯⎯⎯⎯⎯⎯⎯⎯⎯⎯⎯⎯⎯⎯⎯⎯⎯

   c. My likely choice of degree objective for career preparation at this college: ☐ Associate ☐ Bachelor's in:

   ⎯⎯⎯⎯⎯⎯⎯⎯⎯⎯⎯⎯⎯⎯⎯⎯⎯⎯⎯⎯⎯⎯⎯⎯⎯⎯⎯⎯⎯⎯⎯⎯

   Notes: ⎯⎯⎯⎯⎯⎯⎯⎯⎯⎯⎯⎯⎯⎯⎯⎯⎯⎯⎯⎯⎯⎯⎯⎯⎯⎯⎯⎯⎯

   ⎯⎯⎯⎯⎯⎯⎯⎯⎯⎯⎯⎯⎯⎯⎯⎯⎯⎯⎯⎯⎯⎯⎯⎯⎯⎯⎯⎯⎯⎯⎯⎯

   ⎯⎯⎯⎯⎯⎯⎯⎯⎯⎯⎯⎯⎯⎯⎯⎯⎯⎯⎯⎯⎯⎯⎯⎯⎯⎯⎯⎯⎯⎯⎯⎯

   d. Possible other advantages/drawbacks for my career preparation:

   ⎯⎯⎯⎯⎯⎯⎯⎯⎯⎯⎯⎯⎯⎯⎯⎯⎯⎯⎯⎯⎯⎯⎯⎯⎯⎯⎯⎯⎯⎯⎯⎯

   ⎯⎯⎯⎯⎯⎯⎯⎯⎯⎯⎯⎯⎯⎯⎯⎯⎯⎯⎯⎯⎯⎯⎯⎯⎯⎯⎯⎯⎯⎯⎯⎯

2. **My other aims—extent to which I could realize my goals in:**
   a. Skills development: ⎯⎯⎯⎯⎯⎯⎯⎯⎯⎯⎯⎯⎯⎯⎯⎯⎯⎯⎯⎯
   b. Personal development: ⎯⎯⎯⎯⎯⎯⎯⎯⎯⎯⎯⎯⎯⎯⎯⎯⎯⎯
   c. Greater understanding: ⎯⎯⎯⎯⎯⎯⎯⎯⎯⎯⎯⎯⎯⎯⎯⎯⎯⎯
   d. Personal enjoyment: ⎯⎯⎯⎯⎯⎯⎯⎯⎯⎯⎯⎯⎯⎯⎯⎯⎯⎯⎯

continued on next page

48

WORKSHEET 4. EVALUATION OF A COLLEGE'S INFORMATION (*continued*)

3. Extent to which the college provides other services I want:
   a. Career planning and counseling: _____
   b. Job placement: _____
   c. Review and refresher sessions for adjusting to studies: _____
_____
   d. Help with developing good study skills: _____
   e. Child-care services: _____
   f. Other services: _____
_____
_____

Key Factors—How Satisfactory Are They for Me?

1. Basic feasibility for me in (check each if practical):
   ☐ Attendance schedule. Notes: _____
   ☐ Location. Notes: _____
_____
_____
   ☐ Admissions requirements. Notes: _____
_____
_____
   ☐ Costs. Notes: _____
_____

2. Institutional accreditation of the college:
   ☐ State accreditation
   ☐ Regional accreditation
   ☐ Programs that hold professional accreditation (list any that may be of special interest to me):
_____
_____

3. Any other marked advantages or drawbacks of the college or program:
_____
_____
_____

called terminal programs. If you plan a transfer program, make sure all your credits will be accepted at your future bachelor's degree college by consulting with that college when you start planning your associate degree program.

3. Community colleges usually have the least demanding admissions requirements and the lowest tuition costs in their locales, in keeping with their mission of serving the community.

Therefore, your options with associate degree programs include a terminal program to prepare you for your immediate career goals; a transfer program to serve as an economical first half of a bachelor's program preparing you for your career field; and an inexpensive, flexible program to let you begin your studies while you are still determining your career goals and keeping your decision open to pursue either an associate or a bachelor's degree.

Analyze College Information for Advantages beyond Career Goals

Check the literature of each college to see how that college or program can help you realize the advantages you seek in the other areas you identified in your Advantage Inventory. These include the following:

- skills development in specific areas
- personal development
- greater understanding
- personal enjoyment or enrichment in cultural experience

Look for Key Services

Find out from the college literature whether a college you're considering provides helpful services such as:

- Career counseling
- Job placement of graduates
- Refresher sessions to brush up on rusty academic skills
- Help with developing study skills in order to earn passing or high marks
- Child-care services at low or no cost

Note in item 3 of your evaluation worksheet any other useful services mentioned in the literature of a college you're considering.

Evaluate Information on Such Key Factors as Practicality and Accreditation

Two key feasibility factors in your choice of a college and program are the attendance schedule and the convenience of location. Both are simple factors to evaluate. A quick look at a school's schedule can tell you if the required class sessions are workable for you, and the school's location will determine whether you can commute to it with little or no difficulty.

Investigate Admissions Requirements

Many degree programs designed especially for adult students have liberal admissions requirements. Anyone who wishes to enroll may usually do so. Of course the student must then demonstrate sufficient ability to complete the coursework with passing grades.

A number of programs for adults even waive the common college admissions requirement of high school graduation. Those programs typically state that the admission of a student without a high school diploma is provisional until he or she successfully completes some specified number of credits, usually between 15 and 30.

Although you are not likely to find it difficult to gain admission to a program that meets your needs in other areas, you should look carefully at each college's statement on admissions requirements to be certain you can meet them. Note on Worksheet 4 any deadline dates you may have to meet and look for specific requirements that might categorically exclude you. For instance, a few programs are open only to residents of certain states or only to women or only to persons of a certain minimum age like 22 or 25.

Also note on the worksheet what you need to do to meet the requirements or recommendations for admission, such as:

- Supplying a transcript of your high school studies, a transcript of any college courses, and similar official records of any coursework taken outside of high school or college
- Filing a completed application blank (which may have been included in the college material you requested
- Taking one or more specified tests

Assume that you will do well enough to qualify for admission on any tests that may be required, even though you may feel unsure of your test-taking ability. Admissions tests in programs for adult students are generally used for academic guidance in beginning coursework rather than for admission.

Judge Feasibility in Terms of Total Costs

One of the most significant questions to examine at the outset is the cost of a particular college or program. Tuition and fees for some colleges and programs might make them impractically expensive compared with other college opportunities open to you.

To see roughly what your costs in a program would run, use the Estimate of Degree-Study Costs per Year (Worksheet 5). As it indicates, there are

WORKSHEET 5. ESTIMATE OF DEGREE-STUDY COSTS PER YEAR AT:

_____

(name of college)

1. Tuition and fees (per year)

Number of credits I take in a typical year: _____
  Multiplied by tuition charge per credit
    ($_____ per credit): $_____
Additional fees
  Registration per term ($_____)
    multiplied by number of terms a year (_____)
    I register for: $_____
  Other fees (library, health, student activities),
    total per year: $_____

  Total fees per year $_____

2. Books and supplies (per year)

Estimate at about $10 per credit for which you enroll: $_____

3. Travel to classes (per year)

Bus/train subway fares per week ($_____)
  multiplied by number of weeks per year classes
  meet (_____; often about 35): $_____
OR out-of-pocket auto travel costs
  Gasoline per week ($_____)
  multiplied by number of weeks per year classes
  meet (_____):   _____
Tolls and parking per week ($_____)
  multiplied by number of weeks
  per year (_____):   _____

  Total auto travel costs per year $_____

continued on next page

WORKSHEET 5. ESTIMATE OF DEGREE-STUDY
COSTS PER YEAR AT: (*continued*)

(name of college)

4. Incidentals (per year)

Restaurant snacks or meals (due to classes)
per week $_____;
per year: $_____
Baby-sitter or other child-care costs
per week $_____;
per year: $_____
Possible special equipment costs
typewriter $_____
calculator $_____
other_____ $_____

_____
_____
_____

Total equipment costs $_____
Miscellaneous other costs
_____ $_____
_____ $_____
_____ $_____
_____ $_____

Total miscellaneous $_____

Total incidentals $_____

Grand total costs per year $_____

four major types of expenses you incur in studying for a degree:

1. Tuition and fees
2. Books and supplies
3. Travel to classes
4. Incidentals

Total costs for tuition and fees are likely to vary substantially among colleges. Other types of costs would probably differ only to a minor extent from one college to another (unless your travel costs were abnormally high for a college very far away, or abnormally low for a college within walking distance).

All major costs are included in the worksheet to help you get a complete picture of what your actual expenses are likely to be. You can use this form to help figure your expense budget for college every year. Only its "special equipment" items are one-time expenses that won't recur in subsequent years.

Tuition and Fees. The following comments and examples related to tuition and fees will help you use the estimate worksheet to figure these major cost items correctly.

Tuition charges for the part-time study programs typically taken by adult students are set on a per-credit basis and thus correspond directly to the credit value of each course for which you register each term. Look in the college's literature for specific programs that interest you. To see how many credits you would take per year, add the credits you'd probably take per term and multiply by the number of terms per year. Some colleges divide the school year into two semesters, others into three quarters, plus perhaps a summer session and one or more short intersessions.

Then, multiply the total probable credits taken per year by the college's tuition charge per credit for that program and for your status as a student. (Out-of-state residents typically pay more at public colleges; students over age 65 are entitled to lower rates at a number of colleges.) Note the following three examples of typical tuition and fee costs per year for 1984–85.

One of the more than 30 community colleges in New York State (comparatively high-cost community colleges)

Number of credits (semester hours) per year: 20 (8 per semester plus 4 summer)
Tuition per credit for a New York State resident for part-time study (fewer than 12 credits): $47.50

Tuition per year (20 credits times $47.50 per credit):	$ 950.00
Fees per year ($20.05 per term, times 3 terms):	60.15
Total tuition and fees per year	$1,010.15

School of Continuing Education, New York University (private university of moderately high cost)

Number of credits per year: 20 (10 per semester)
Tuition per semester (flat fee for part-time study,
6 to 10 credits): $1,772

Tuition per year ($1,772 times 2 semesters):	$3,544.00
Fees per year ($68 per semester, times 2 semesters):	136.00
Total tuition and fees per year	$3,680.00

Weekend College, Central Missouri State University

Number of credits per year: 20 (10 per semester)
Tuition per credit (same for in-state and out-of-state residents; higher at off-campus centers): $45

Tuition per year (20 credits times $45 per credit):	$900.00
Total fees per term:	0.00
Total tuition and fees per year	$900.00

For figuring your yearly costs other than tuition and fees, Worksheet 5 is largely self-explanatory. At this time don't completely rule out any one program or college only on the basis of high cost. If a high-cost college or program has some unique advantages for you, keep it in reserve. Financial aid, covered in chapter 5, might make it workable.

Accreditation Status

The next key factor to be evaluated on Worksheet 4 is accreditation. See what the college reports in its literature. Then consult one of the separate sources on regional accreditation previously mentioned to verify whether or not the college has it. You can assume the college holds state accreditation if it is in operation.

If professional accreditation of study programs is of special interest to you, include that information on the worksheet.

Other Major Pluses or Minuses

In the last section of Worksheet 4 note other important factors about the program and college that you consider either a marked attraction or a drawback. For example, the advantages might include use of the campus gym and Olympic-size swimming pool, or special programs in the arts or computers that appeal to you. Minuses might be a school's location in an unsafe neighborhood or the lack of convenient parking facilities.

Visit Promising Colleges for Interviews and Firsthand Inspection

Once you've carefully evaluated the information you've gotten by mail, arrange to visit each college that appears unusually promising. Make an appointment for the visit by telephoning the admissions office. Your appointment will probably be with one of the admissions counselors who confer with prospective students. Or you may be given an appointment with some other admissions office staff member serving much the same function.

Plan to arrive a half hour or more before the appointed time. Use that extra time to examine the college's complete catalog and any additional informational publications you did not receive by mail.

What to Cover in Your First Interview with a College Admissions Counselor

Make the most of your first meeting with the admissions counselor. Use the Admissions Counselor Questions Checklist (Worksheet 6) as a guide. It covers the basic questions to ask in your interview. Raise any other questions and discuss to your satisfaction any further points these questions may lead to. Make several copies of the checklist and bring one to each interview. It will be a useful reference both during and after the interview.

How to Handle College Visits and Interviews

In your meeting with an admissions counselor (or admissions staff member) at a college, the counselor should help with all of your questions and requests insofar as her or his knowledge and time permit. Arrange to see as many of the campus features covered on the checklist as possible, and set up as many interviews as possible with others connected with the college.

At any college you should be able to inspect most of the campus features indicated on the checklist. Some colleges offer campus tours conducted for groups of prospective students by current students who serve as volunteer guides. Even without a formal tour, you can find your own way around the campus with directions on where to go and a campus map that most colleges provide. You might also need a pass to show to campus security guards.

Some colleges do not allow visitors to sit in on actual class sessions or to have interviews with staff members in the areas of financial aid, academic advisory services, or career placement services before they become registered students. This tends to be the rule at community and state colleges laboring to provide low-cost opportunities in the face of heavy work loads and limited monetary support from their sponsoring local and state governments.

WORKSHEET 6. ADMISSIONS COUNSELOR
QUESTIONS CHECKLIST

1. My Admission

☐ In view of my background (report on it), do you see any problem I might have in being admitted to the program of study I'm considering?

☐ If so, what might I do to resolve it? (Ask this in reference to each possible problem.)

2. My Program of Study

☐ In view of my career goals and other aims (describe them), do you think the program I'm considering is the right one?

☐ Could you explain why? (Get answers for each major aim.)

☐ If not the right one, what might be a better alternative for me?

☐ How might I structure my coursework in the program I'm considering to take the best advantage of what it has to offer me?

3. College Services I Might Want to Draw On

☐ After I'm admitted, will I be able to get help in planning my choice of courses and my course schedule during the registration period for my first term of study? Just how might such advice work for me?

☐ May I consult an academic adviser if I have problems or questions with my studies after I begin my courses? Who might that person be, and when might I meet with him or her?

Does the college offer the following services?

☐ Help in developing my study skills or academic abilities; tutoring services

☐ Career planning services (to help me make or refine my career plans)

☐ Job placement services near the time I'll be graduating

☐ Child-care services

☐ Access to sports facilities and activities (gym, swimming pool, playing fields, recreational team sports, tennis courts, etc.)

☐ Parking privileges

☐ Other: _____

☐ _____

☐ _____

WORKSHEET 6. ADMISSIONS COUNSELOR
QUESTIONS CHECKLIST

4. Possible Degree Credit for My Previous Learning

☐ Are there possibilities for receiving degree credit for my previous learning in addition to those described in the college's literature? (Say what those ways are.)

☐ What are the specific procedures I should use to apply for and be granted such credits?

☐ What is the maximum number of credits for previous learning and credits by examination I can receive toward my degree?

☐ Do I understand correctly that the charges for being granted credits for previous learning are those indicated in the college's literature? (Say what they are.)

5. Financial Aid and Costs Charged by the College

☐ Here's the financial aid I hope to apply for (describe it). What do you think my chances are for receiving aid of each type?

☐ Are there other possible kinds of aid I should try for?

☐ Here's my estimate of tuition costs and other fees I would be charged per year for the number of credits I'm likely to take in the program of study I'm considering (tell or show what your estimates are). Have I left anything out, or made any mistakes?

6. Career Planning and Job Placement Services

☐ Are there services and other offerings in career planning and job placement available to me beyond those described in the college's catalog? (Identify those.)

☐ Have graduates of the program I'm considering been successful in finding jobs in their field?

☐ Do you have any figures on the percentage of graduates who have gotten jobs in this career field by, say, a month after receiving their degrees?

7. Visiting the College in Session

Would it be possible to arrange for me to see the following college areas or activities in normal operation?

☐ Two or three types of classes in the program I'm considering?

☐ Laboratory rooms or special equipment used in courses in the program?

continued on next page

58

WORKSHEET 6. ADMISSIONS COUNSELOR
QUESTIONS CHECKLIST (*continued*)

☐ The college library facilities available to students? What evening and weekend hours is the library open during the academic year?

☐ Student lounges, or the student center or student union, that I could use as an enrolled student? What evening and weekend hours are these student facilities open?

☐ Student snack bar or dining halls? Could I have a meal there as a visitor?

☐ Sports facilities open to students in the program I'm considering? What hours would I be allowed to use them?

☐ Child-care or nursery school facilities available to students' children?

Other college offices where I might seek help as a student?

☐ Financial Aid Office.
☐ Career Services and Job Placement Office.
☐ Academic adviser's office.
☐ Office of the director of the program I'm considering.
☐ Office of the dean or director of the division or college in which the program I'm considering operates.
☐ Any other main features of the campus buildings or grounds of possible interest or importance to me that you suggest. Notes on suggestions: _____

_____

☐ Any neighborhood features of interest or importance that you suggest (coffee shops, photocopying stores, shopping centers, parks, museums, parking lots, etc.). Notes on suggestions: _____

_____

8. **Other college staff members with whom I might arrange to confer briefly, if possible**

☐ An instructor or a professor in the program I'm considering (perhaps the person whose class I visit).

☐ Career Planning/Services/Placement Office staff member (or staff members, if handled in two or more separate offices).

☐ Financial Aid Office staff member.

☐ Two or three students now enrolled in the program I'm considering.

☐ Two or three recent graduates of the program who are now working in my intended career field.

In your meeting with a financial aid office staff member, talk in more detail about questions in section 5 of Worksheet 6, the Admissions Counselor Questions Checklist.

In your meeting with a career services office staff member, use section 2 and section 6 of the checklist.

The following are suggested questions to ask other members of the college community. Feel free to add to and modify this list, based on your own needs. In approaching any of these people, introduce yourself as someone seriously thinking of enrolling as a student.

Suggested Questions for a College's Faculty Members, Students, and Graduates Working in the Intended Career Field

---

Professors or Instructors

1. What are the main things you would advise me to do to get the most out of my courses here, once I enroll?
2. How much time should I plan to spend on study and assignments outside of class for every hour spent in class?
3. Is course grading at the college based on the curve (the bell-shaped curve of normal distribution), or is it based on fixed academic standards regardless of the ability level of the students in any particular class?
4. How are grades for differing kinds of student work in a course weighted in arriving at a final grade? For instance, are they weighted one-third for class participation, one-third for papers or projects done outside the class, and one-third for the average of midterm and final examinations?
5. What's the range of class size? How would my classes generally be taught—by the lecture method, the lecture-discussion method, or the seminar method?
6. Do you have regularly scheduled office hours for conferences with students enrolled in your courses? Would the same usually be true for faculty members teaching other courses?
7. If I needed substantial extra help with my studies in your class, how could I get it? From tutoring arrangements? From a learning skills center or other service at the college? In some special noncredit courses like ones on overcoming math anxiety, or faster reading and note taking, or effective writing skills?

Current Students in My Intended Study Program

1. How do you like the college? What do you like best about it? What do you like least about it?

2. How did you happen to pick the study program you're in?
3. What courses and teachers do you like best? Least?
4. Based on your experience, what problems might I run into if I enrolled in the same program, and how could I avoid them, if possible?
5. How have you found the college's services in [pick ones most important to you] financial aid? career planning? academic advising? study skills development? others?

Recent Graduates of the Study Program Working in My Intended Career Field

1. How well did the study program prepare you for getting a job? For doing the work and winning advancement in the career?
2. How effective were the college's career services or job placement staff members in helping you find and get a job?
3. What would you suggest that I do to get the most out of the program as a student?
4. Can you alert me to any problems I might run into as a student, and how I might avoid them?

Persist in finding out what can help you most. In gathering information about a college, follow up any indications of services or program options that might be of unusual benefit to you. Making persistent inquiries in various college offices and carefully reading bulletins may uncover attractive possibilities. Talking with students can also acquaint you with helpful aspects of the college you hadn't learned of from other sources. A counselor or other staff member may not think of every course offering or special service that would be beneficial to your situation.

Be equally persistent after you enroll at a college. You'll have at least several terms to take advantage of helpful features you discover as you go along.

Make Your Final Comparisons of Colleges

Try to make in-depth investigations of two or more colleges. Do so even if only one of the colleges that interest you is located in your vicinity. Explore the possibility of getting your degree from a distant college that requires little or no class attendance. You can gather the necessary information by analyzing the college's bulletins and by letters or phone calls.

After you have compared the various promising colleges, one institution may seem far and away the best choice for you. That happens for some students. For others, it's hard to decide among several alternative colleges. If that's true in your case, the scale in Worksheet 7 may prove helpful. It's a method of summing up the merits of each of a number of comparable colleges to determine which is best for you.

The scale in Worksheet 7 is designed to rank individual college features numerically. The numbers are then tallied to determine which college has the best score. Based on your investigations, write in the numerical rank of a given feature for each college compared with the other colleges you're considering. Use a ranking scale in which 1 is best and 2, 3, 4, etc. are successively less desirable. For example, suppose you're comparing four colleges: Bayview, Community, Dawson, and State. First, fill in their names on the top-line blanks. Then, for feature *A*, give rankings based on your judgments. You might assign rankings as follows: Community—1, Bayview—2, State—3, and Dawson—4. You fill in those rank numbers accordingly for feature *A*. Similarly assign rank-order values for each of the other features.

Here is part of the worksheet filled in for the four hypothetical colleges, to show how you might enter your own rank-order decisions.

College Feature	*Names of colleges (enter rank order for each in columns)*			
	Bayview C.	*Community C.*	*Dawson U.*	*State U.*
A. Program that best realizes career and other goals	2	1	4	3
B. Most convenient attendance schedule/sites	1	3	2	4
C. Lowest cost and highest financial aid mix	4	1	3	2
Total	7	5	9	9

WORKSHEET 7. RANK-ORDER SCALE FOR COMPARING COLLEGES

College Feature	Names of colleges (enter rank order for each in columns)			
A. Program that best realizes career and other goals	_____	_____	_____	_____
B. Most convenient attendance schedule/sites	_____	_____	_____	_____
C. Lowest cost and highest financial aid mix	_____	_____	_____	_____
D. Most credit for prior learning	_____	_____	_____	_____
E. Shortest total time to finish study for degree	_____	_____	_____	_____
F. Best for career preparation and job placement	_____	_____	_____	_____
G. Best on-campus support services	_____	_____	_____	_____

63

WORKSHEET 7. RANK-ORDER SCALE FOR COMPARING COLLEGES

College Feature *Names of colleges (enter rank order for each in columns)*

_____ _____ _____ _____

H. Best overall
reputation for
quality (op-
tional)

_____ _____ _____ _____

Others you want:

I. _____ _____ _____ _____ _____

J. _____ _____ _____ _____ _____

K. _____ _____ _____ _____ _____

L. _____ _____ _____ _____ _____

M. _____ _____ _____ _____ _____

Total _____ _____ _____ _____

You can see from the shortened example on p. 61 how the scales can help you reach a decision. Adding each column gives you totals that combine the factors. The lowest total number indicates the college that has the highest combined standing on all the advantages you're looking for.

As you see, in this numerical evaluation Community College ranks highest in combined advantages, and Bayview College stands second. Dawson and State universities are two points behind Bayview, with equal standings.

You can adapt such scales as you wish. For instance, if features A and C are twice as important to you as the other features, give double weight to those features (by dividing each of the 1-to-4 rank numbers for these features by 2) before tallying the points for all features.

You may use the scale to help you see the colleges in perspective, but then overrule the numbers and make your final decision on the basis of your subjective judgments. Many people pick a college for emotional as well as practical reasons. The important aim is for you to make well-informed choices rather than to select blindly.

How to Apply to a Competitive College

Most college programs designed for adults have fairly open admissions policies. Some, however, have many more applicants than they can accommodate and therefore cannot accept all qualified persons who apply for admission. In those situations students compete with each other for acceptance, and even some who are well qualified are rejected.

Questions suggested for your interview with college admissions counselors should uncover any programs with competitive admissions among those you're considering. Answers to those questions should prove a fairly reliable guide to your chances of acceptance.

In competitive admissions there is always the possibility of rejection, however strong your qualifications. You can't tell in advance how strong other applicants may be or what subjective factors might come into play when your application is evaluated. Go ahead and apply to a competitive study program that offers distinct advantages, but be sure to apply to at least one other program that interests you and assures you admission.

5. Financing College with Your Resources and Financial Aid

Like many adults who go to college while working, you will probably finance most of your college costs out of your own earnings, savings, other resources, or loans. However, some financial aid for college is available to adults who have extreme need for aid. Other adults who attend on at least a half-time basis may also qualify for some aid. This chapter summarizes how you can make the most of your own resources and any possibilities for financial aid.

When to Start Financial Planning for College

Start finding out about costs and financial aid possibilities as soon as you start collecting information about colleges. Once you've chosen a college, you're ready to decide when to enroll. Choose a term that leaves you enough time to organize your home and work schedules and meet all the college's admissions requirements. A fall term beginning in September is the traditional time for initial enrollment. But many colleges and programs for adults permit entrance at the beginning of the spring semester or summer session.

Depending on your college's application deadline and other requirements, it will take you anywhere from a month to six or eight months to meet all admissions requirements. If an application form and a high school transcript are the only documents required, allow about a month for preparation. This should also allow a bare minimum of time for applying for financial aid.

Plan on six to eight months, however, to meet the extensive admissions and financial aid application requirements set by some colleges. These can include application deadlines four to eight months before the term begins, scores on college entrance tests that require advance registration, written recommendations, transcripts of all prior studies, and detailed financial aid forms. (How to cope with such requirements is explained in chapter 6.)

A number of colleges with extensive requirements admit new students only in the fall term. In aiming for such a college, start the application procedure no later than eight or nine months preceding the September in which you want to enroll.

Ideally, start exploring and planning for college and financial aid in late fall or early winter of any year with an eye to entering classes the following fall. Such planning is particularly important for adult students who need substantial amounts of financial aid. Adults who need little or no financial aid, and are applying to noncompetitive colleges, can start as late as a month before the term begins.

How to Finance College Studies

The following accounts illustrate how several typical working adults are currently financing their college studies. Each case describes the student's college expense budget and the combined personal resources and financial aid that cover those expenses. One of these cases may parallel your own situation closely enough to serve as a guide for you.

Married Homemaker Studies to Become Teacher

In her mid-thirties, Barbara Walsh has begun taking part-time day and evening college classes to become a state-certified elementary school teacher. Her son and daughter are in junior high school and no longer need as much of her time as when they were younger. It is important to her to prepare for an employed career that has long attracted her and to increase the family's income.

Through careful inquiries she's learned that in her suburban New England area, a long, steady increase in elementary school enrollments is projected, with a rising demand for elementary schoolteachers. While majoring in elementary education for her bachelor's degree, she also plans to take a minor in helping children with learning disabilities—a specialty in particularly high demand.

At the private university she attends for 20 hours a week, tuition charges are $172 per semester-hour credit, and her fees per semester run $64. Gasoline costs about $5 a week, but there are no parking fees at the university. Incidental expenses are few: she estimates a dollar a week for snacks. Her total expense budget is as follows, using the Estimate of Degree-Study Costs per Year (Worksheet 5 in chapter 4).

1. **Tuition and fees (per year)**
   Number of credits I take in a typical year: ___20___
   Multiplied by tuition charge per credit ($__172__ per credit) $__3,440__
   Additional fees
   Registration per term ($__64__) multiplied by number
   of terms a year (__2__) I register for: $___128___
   Other fees (library, health, student activities),
   total per year: $_____
   Total fees per year $___128___

2. **Books and supplies (per year)**
   Estimate at about $10 per credit for which you enroll $___200___

3. **Travel to classes (per year)**
   Bus/train/subway fares per week ($_____) multiplied
   by number of weeks per year classes meet (_____;
   often about 35) $_____
   OR out-of-pocket auto travel costs
   Gasoline per week ($__5__) multiplied by number
   of weeks per year classes meet (__35__): $___175___
   Tolls and parking per week ($_____) multiplied
   by number of weeks per year (_____): $_____
   Total auto travel costs per year $___175___

4. **Incidentals (per year)**
   Restaurant snacks or meals (due to classes)
   per week $__1__;
   per year: $__35__
   Baby-sitter or other child-care costs
   per week $_____;
   per year: $_____
   Possible special equipment costs
   typewriter $_____
   calculator $_____
   other _____
   _____ $_____
   Total equipment costs $_____

Miscellaneous other costs

_____ $_____

_____ $_____

_____ $_____

Total miscellaneous $_____

Total incidentals $___35___

Grand total costs per year $_____3,978____

Barbara's husband, Jim, is a head bank teller with an after-tax income of $288 a week, or about $15,000 a year. Barbara gets the money to cover her total annual college costs of $3,978 as follows:

$50.55 a week saved from family income (plan started
    six months in advance) $2,628.60
Guaranteed Student Loan (in her name)   1,350.00
    Total resources per year $3,978.60

Barbara had finished her first year of college (30 credits) before she and Jim were married. She also has started to earn credits by taking selected exams, which require additional studying, and plans to get prior-learning credit for her past training and experience as a volunteer teaching English to inner-city Hispanics and Orientals. The accumulated credits will account for some 60 of the 120 needed for her degree, she has been told by her Wellington University advisers.

She plans to take 20 credits per year for three years. Her Guaranteed Student Loan (GSL) obligations will total approximately $4,300 (including 6 percent origination and insurance fees of $81 per $1,350 borrowed annually). The repayment burden will be manageable, she figures, running $50 a month for about nine years.

The Guaranteed Student Loan Program is a widely used form of college student aid. These federally guaranteed loans carry no interest while the student is in college; a subsidized 8 percent (in 1985) simple interest is applied once repayment begins six months after the student leaves college or completes studies. Ask about these loans and other possible federal and state aid at a college's financial aid office. Interest and other terms on which you take out GSLs can vary from year to year. There may be restrictions for part-time study or income ceilings.

Father Prepares for Career Change

At age 38, Ron Zimmer has decided to head in a new career direction. His two earlier occupations didn't offer him a secure future. Now he is determined to do all he can to guarantee his prospects for job security and a good income. He is studying for his bachelor's degree with a major in accounting because he's found that job demand, incomes, and future prospects are all favorable for accountants. He has also discovered an aptitude for and an interest in working with figures that involve money.

Beyond getting his bachelor's with an accounting major, Ron has two further goals in mind to guarantee job success. One is to take a computer science minor because accounting and computer skills make an especially strong combination in the job market. His second goal is to prepare as effectively as possible for the Certified Public Accountant (C.P.A.) examinations after getting his degree; C.P.A.s generally have the best prospects and the highest incomes in the accounting profession.

In his younger years, Ron thought he could get along fine without a college education. After high school he worked with his dad and neighborhood friends at the auto assembly plant in town. He was making good money and having a great time right from the start. He and Ginnie settled down and had their three boys over the next few years.

Then came the slump in the auto industry and layoffs at the plant. Ron was let go. Fortunately his experience in auto body repair work helped Ron land a job as an auto insurance claims adjuster.

Claims adjusting didn't pay as well as the auto assembly plant had. It also didn't offer much opportunity for advancement. He might be promoted to supervisor, but not much beyond. At the assembly plant and in the insurance company, he had seen that the people with college degrees were the ones who moved into executive jobs. Fair or not, it just wasn't enough to be a hard-working employee with good ideas. Many other hard-working employees with good ideas were also college graduates.

Ron decided to enroll in a program at the large state university in a nearby city. Its business school offered a part-time program for adults leading to a bachelor's degree with accounting as one of the available majors. His first-year expense budget follows (using Worksheet 5).

For: Ron Zimmer

Estimate of Degree-Study Costs per Year

1. *Tuition and fees (per year)*
   25 credits (including summer session) at $37 per credit $ 925
   Fees   216
2. *Books and supplies (per year)*
   25 credits times $10 per credit (estimate)   250
3. *Travel to classes (per year)*
   43 weeks at $8 per week   344
4. *Incidentals (per year)*   258
   Total costs per year $1,993

Ron's employer is one of the largest insurance firms in the country. Like many large corporations, the company has a tuition-aid plan as part of its employee benefits. The plan is generous, covering the costs of tuition and related fees for any degree-credit studies passed by the employee. Ron is reimbursed for the costs of his tuition and related fees each term after he completes his coursework with passing or better marks.

Ron's financial resources for paying his college costs for the year are as follows:

Reimbursement by employer's tuition aid plan	$1,141
$16.40 a week saved from family income	852
Total resources per year	$1,993

Ron and his advisers estimate it will take him about five years of part-time study to earn his bachelor's degree. His supervisor at work is impressed with Ron's ambition, and the personnel manager has indicated that he will be offered an accounting job at a competitive salary once he gets his degree.

Supermarket Cashier Trains for Nursing Career

Sue Bransky shares an apartment with three other women and works as a checkout clerk at a supermarket that's open 24 hours a day. She had drifted along in various romances and jobs since her high school days without making any plans. Then, at age 29, after breaking up with the man she'd been living with for two years, Sue decided to do something for herself. A friend who was going to the local community college suggested that Sue see an admissions counselor there.

Sue has no money beyond what she earns. But the counselor has helped her plan a way to become better educated for a career she's thought about for a long time—nursing.

Using what the counselor calls a career ladder in nursing, Sue has started a one-year, full-time study program that will accomplish two things. First, it will qualify her as a licensed practical nurse (L.P.N.), earning at least twice the salary she makes at the supermarket. Second, her one-year program completes half the credit requirements for an associate degree program qualifying her for the state registered nurse (R.N.) examination. As an R.N., Sue can hold supervisory positions and make three or four times her supermarket earnings.

Moreover, Sue can work as an L.P.N. while getting her associate degree. And after starting work as a well-paid R.N., she can go on studying part-time for her bachelor's degree in nursing. That will equip her for still better pay with more responsibility.

She can even go on from there to earn graduate degrees and become a professor of nursing or a hospital executive. And as a nurse she will be able to work almost anywhere she chooses.

In her first year of L.P.N. studies, Sue prefers to work night shifts at the all-night supermarket and attend school during the day. (The program is also offered in the evening on a part-time study basis.) Her expense budget for the year's degree-credit studies is as follows:

For: Sue Bransky

Estimate of Degree-Study Costs per Year

1. *Tuition and fees (per year)*	
30 credits at $12.50 per credit	$ 375
Fees	80
2. *Books and supplies (per year)*	
30 credits times $10 per credit (estimate)	300
3. *Travel to classes (per year)*	
35 weeks at $6 per week	210
4. *Incidentals (per year)*	70
Total costs per year	$1,035

Some of Sue's expenses are covered by a small state grant for which she qualifies. This financial aid keeps her from having to borrow money. The grant, plus $10 to $15 a week that she squeezes out of her minimum-wage earnings of $110 a week after taxes, is paying her way up the first rung of her nursing career ladder, as the following figures show:

State grant for nursing students	$ 500
$15.30 a week saved from wages (35 weeks)	535
Total resources per year	$1,035

Sue finds it hard to take a full-time study program and keep up in her assignments while also working full-time night hours in the supermarket. Early in the term she could have dropped courses and shifted back to part-time study without a penalty, but now that she has adjusted to the pace, she takes keen satisfaction in being able to handle it all.

Divorced Mother Heads for Career as Business Executive

After finishing two years of college as an English major, Mary Landon had married and gone to work as a secretary to help Hal through law school.

She stopped working in an office when their daughter, Jill, was born. Over the next few years the marriage disintegrated and Mary got a divorce.

At 31, she felt an urge to develop a career and decided to take advantage of increasing opportunities for women to get into management as business executives. A prestigious private college nearby offers to adult students a reentry program that appealed to her. The program has an impressive record of placing graduates in management entry positions with major corporations.

Mary has worked out a study program for a major in economics with a minor in computer science. She and her adviser agree that this should give her a solid grounding to start as an administrative assistant being trained for management. It also provides a good base for possible later study for a Master of Business Administration (M.B.A.), which a future employer might be willing to fund.

Mary is able to take courses during regular 9-to-3 weekday hours because Jill, now 7, is in school. She can study full-time, and plans to get her bachelor's in two years. Her expense budget is as follows:

For: Mary Landon

Estimate of Degree-Study Costs per Year

1. *Tuition and fees (per year)*
   Tuition for full-time study $4,800
   Fees   40
2. *Books and supplies (per year)*   300
3. *Travel to classes (per year)*   250
4. *Incidentals (per year)*   100
      Total costs per year $5,490

Under her divorce settlement, Mary is paid only basic living expenses and child support. Therefore she qualifies as a high-need applicant for financial aid at the college. She receives substantial amounts of yearly need-based aid, as the following budget shows:

Pell Grant (federal aid) $1,500
State grant   500
College grant   1,000
Guaranteed Student Loan (maximum)   2,500
      Total resources per year $5,500

Even with $3,000 a year in grant aid, Mary has to borrow the $2,500 a year maximum permitted undergraduates in the GSL program. She would rather not borrow so heavily, but believes she is justified in order to secure future financial independence and promising career prospects.

Warehouse Foreman Prepares for Retirement
Business in Electronics

Rounding out 40 years as a warehouse worker and foreman with a large retailing chain, Jack Klein looks forward to pursuing two interests after his approaching retirement—running a small business of his own and working with electronic gadgets.

He has long enjoyed being an electronics hobbyist, operating his own ham radio station and doing minor repairs on devices ranging from TVs and stereos to pocket calculators and personal computers. But he now wants to learn electronics systematically and to use that knowledge to open an electronics repair service in the high-demand areas of small computers, color TV sets, video-cassette recorders and cameras, laser-run compact disk phonographs, and video-disk players.

To achieve those goals, Jack has enrolled in an associate degree program in electronics technology at a local community college. His electives include accounting and marketing courses for background in running his small business. His expenses for study are as follows:

For: Jack Klein

Estimate of Degree-Study Costs per Year

1. *Tuition and fees (per year)*

15 credits at $15 per credit (half cost for persons over age 62)	$ 225
Fees	110

2. *Books and supplies (per year)*

15 credits times $10 per credit (estimate)	150

3. *Travel to classes (per year)*

35 weeks at $8 per week	280

4. *Incidentals (per year)*

	100
Total costs per year	$ 865

Jack's earnings and savings cover the fairly modest costs of preparing for his retirement career, and he receives indirect aid in the form of half-cost tuition available to him at the community college. Jack's resources on a yearly basis for his degree-credit studies are as follows:

Savings	$335
$15.15 a week drawn from earnings (35 weeks)	530
Total resources per year	$865

As is often true for working adults, Jack's earned income and accumulated assets like savings and equity in a home make him ineligible for most forms of aid, which are open only to students who demonstrate financial need. Offsetting the lack of direct financial aid is reduced or free tuition for persons aged 60 or more. These benefits are offered by some 1,200 colleges and universities. Lists of such colleges and a booklet on *Learning Opportunities for Older Persons* are available free on request to:

> Institute of Lifelong Learning
> American Association of Retired Persons
> 1909 K Street NW
> Washington, DC 20049

Demonstrating Your Financial Need

Whether you qualify for financial aid depends on whether you can show financial need. How to demonstrate and estimate your need as a college applicant are explained in the next two sections. As a very general rule, you are not eligible for aid if your income exceeds your basic living expenses by roughly the amount that your college studies will cost.

For example, suppose that your after-tax family income is $12,000 a year and that the subsistence costs of housing, food, clothes, and health care for an American family the size of yours total $8,000 a year. Suppose also that your college costs come to $3,500 a year. In such a highly simplified case you have no financial need because calculations show that you can reasonably afford to spend up to $4,000 a year on college costs.

Here are the few main categories of financial aid for which you are generally *not* required to demonstrate financial need as an adult student:

- Employer tuition-aid plans.
- Veterans' education benefits you accumulated in active duty in the United States Armed Forces after 1977 and for which you set up, and contributed to, a savings plan while in service.
- Scholarships from programs sponsored by private organizations (such as companies, foundations, associations, churches, or labor unions).

Most financial aid awards—scholarships, grants, loans, and jobs—are made in aid programs sponsored by the federal government, state governments, and colleges themselves. And generally the amount of aid is directly related to the recipient's financial need—as calculated in official need analysis systems.

Calculating Financial Need

Costs of attendance minus family contribution equals demonstrated financial need, and you are generally eligible for aid equal to the amount of your demonstrated need. Systems developed and operated by organizations such as the College Scholarship Service (CSS) of the College Board, American College Testing (ACT) Program, the Pennsylvania Higher Education Assistance Agency (PHEAA), and the United States Department of Education (DOE) use a common methodology to calculate a student's ability to contribute toward postsecondary education expenses. For a working adult, the estimate of expected contribution is based on the income and assets of the student and the student's spouse, if any.

Each of the four, however, sponsors its own information-gathering form on which applicants for financial aid provide detailed information about their own and their family's financial situation. The information, which is kept confidential, resembles that given on federal income tax returns.

The forms, issued in new editions for each academic year, are the Financial Aid Form (FAF) and the Student Aid Application for California (SAAC) of the College Scholarship Service, the Application for Federal Student Aid of the Department of Education, the Application for Pennsylvania State Grant and Federal Student Aid of PHEAA, and the Family Financial Statement (FFS) of the American College Testing Program. To show you what these forms are like, a sample copy of the FAF for the 1986–87 academic year is included in this section.

You should fill out whichever form you are instructed to complete by the college or program from which you are seeking financial aid. You probably will not have to fill out more than one of these forms in applying for financial aid, even if you are applying for help from multiple sources. Note that you can use the FAF, the SAAC, the FFS, or the PHEAA application to apply for federal student assistance, including Pell Grants, at no additional charge, provided that you check the appropriate box on the form indicating that you want it to be used.

On your form, you will list all of the colleges, state agencies, and private programs from whom you are seeking help. CSS, ACT, or PHEAA will then send a need analysis report about you to each source listed. That way, you need fill out only one form to meet the requirements of a large number of colleges and programs, instead of having to fill out separate forms. Colleges review and often revise the need analysis results in the light of their own policies and additional information they may have collected from applicants, such as recent tax returns.

76

Financial Aid Form—Side I School Year 1986-87

Warning: If you use this form to establish eligibility for federal student aid and you purposely give
false or misleading information. you may get a $10,000 fine, a prison sentence, or both

OO

All students must complete the white sections. ### Section A—Student's Information

1. Student's name _____ Last _____ First _____ M.I.

2. Student's permanent mailing address
(Mail will be sent to this address. See front cover for state abbreviation.)
Number, street, and apartment number _____
City _____ State Zip code

3. Student's social security number ___ – ___ – ___

4. Student's date of birth Month Day Year

5. Student's home telephone Area Code Number

6. Student's state of legal residence State

7. The student is 1 ☐ a U.S. citizen
2 ☐ an eligible noncitizen (See instructions.)
3 ☐ neither of the above (See instructions.)

8. Student's expected year in college during 1986-87. (Check only one box.)
1 ☐ 1st
2 ☐ 2nd
3 ☐ 3rd
4 ☐ 4th
5 ☐ 5th or more (undergraduate)
6 ☐ first year graduate or professional (beyond a bachelor's degree)
7 ☐ continuing graduate or professional

9. Student's sex (optional)
1 ☐ Male 2 ☐ Female

10. Will the student have a first bachelor's degree by July 1, 1986?
1 ☐ Yes 2 ☐ No

11. The student is 1 ☐ unmarried (single, divorced, or widowed)
2 ☐ married
3 ☐ separated

12. Will the student's spouse be attending college at least half-time during 1986-87?
1 ☐ Yes
2 ☐ No
3 ☐ Student unmarried

13. During the 1986-87 school year, student wants financial aid
from: Month Year
through: Month Year

14. Student's high school code number
(If an entering first-time student during 1986-87. write in your high school 6-digit code number. See instructions.)
High school code no.

Section B—Student's (and Spouse's) Expected Income and Benefits

Summer 1986   School Year 1986-87

15. a. Student's taxable income (Don't include financial aid such as College Work-Study earnings.) 3 months $ _____ .00   9 months $ _____ .00

b. Spouse's taxable income (Don't include financial aid such as College Work-Study earnings.) 3 months $ _____ .00   9 months $ _____ .00

July 1, 1986–June 30, 1987

16. Student's veterans GI Bill and Dependents Educational Assistance Benefits   Amount per month $ _____ .00   Number of months ___

17. Student's veterans VA Contributory Benefits (VEAP)   Amount per month $ _____ .00   Number of months ___

18. Other untaxed income and benefits of student (and spouse)
(Don't include any of the income or benefits given in 15, 16, and 17 or financial aid.)   July 1, 1986–June 30, 1987 $ _____ .00

Section C—Student's Status

Read the instructions to find out who counts as the student's parent(s) before you answer 19, 20, and 21. If you leave any answer blank, it will be counted as "Yes."

	Yes	No		Yes	No
19. Did or will the student live with the parents for more than six weeks (42 days)	. . in 1985? 1 ☐ 2 ☐		. . in 1986? 1 ☐ 2 ☐		
20. Did or will the parents claim the student as a U.S. income tax exemption	. . in 1985? 1 ☐ 2 ☐		. . in 1986? 1 ☐ 2 ☐		
21. Did or will the student get more than $750 worth of support from the parents	. . in 1985? 1 ☐ 2 ☐		. . in 1986? 1 ☐ 2 ☐		

22. If you answered "Yes" to any of the questions in Section C, you must fill in the blue shaded areas.

- **Exception:** If you are married, fill in both the **blue** and the **gray** shaded areas and if you were born after May 31, 1964, have one of your parents sign the **Student Status Certification.** ➡
- If your parents are separated or divorced, if your parent is widowed or single, or if you have a stepparent, you must read the instructions before going on

22. If you answered "No" to all 6 questions in Section C, you must fill in the gray shaded areas. Some colleges or programs may also ask you to fill in the blue shaded areas.

Student Status Certification: If you were born after May 31, 1964 are required to fill out the **gray** shaded areas and have one of your parents certify by signing below that the answers to 19, 20, and 21 are true.

The information in questions 19, 20, and 21 is true to the best of my knowledge. (Proof such as tax forms may be requested.)

_____
Parent's signature

Section D—Household Information

———— Parents ————

23a. Number of family members in 1986-87
(Write in the total number of people that your parents will support in 1986-87. Always include the student. Also, include parents and parents' other dependent children. Include other people only if they meet the definition in the instructions.) You must also give information in 56 on Side II of this form.

23b. Number of college students in 1986-87
(Of the number in 23a, write in the number of family members who will be in college at least half-time. Include the student who is applying for aid.)

23c. Number of parents in college in 1986-87
(Check one box.)
1 ☐ No parent will be in college at least half-time.
2 ☐ One parent will be in college at least half-time.
3 ☐ Both parents will be in college at least half-time.

23d. Parents' current marital status is
1 ☐ single
2 ☐ married
3 ☐ separated
4 ☐ divorced
5 ☐ widowed

23e. Age of the older parent is

23f. Parents' state of legal residence is

———— Student (and spouse) ————

23a. Number of family members in 1986-87
(Write in the total number of people that you and your spouse will support in 1986-87. Include yourself, your spouse, and your dependent children. Include other people only if they meet the definition in the instructions.) You must also give information in 56 on Side II of this form.

23b. Number of college students in 1986-87
(Of the number in 23a, write in the number of family members who will be in college at least half-time. Include yourself (the student who is applying for aid) and others who will be in college at least half-time.)

Section E—Income and Expense Information

		Parents	Student (and spouse)

24. The following 1985 U.S. income tax return figures are (See instructions.)

Parents:
24. 1 ☐ from a completed return. Go to **25.**
2 ☐ estimated. Go to **25.**
3 ☐ a tax return will not be filed. Skip to **30.**

Student (and spouse):
24. 1 ☐ from a completed return. Go to **25.**
2 ☐ estimated. Go to **25.**
3 ☐ a tax return will not be filed. Skip to **30.**

(Tax Filers Only)

25. 1985 total number of exemptions (IRS Form 1040–line 6f, 1040A–line 5f, or 1040EZ–write in "01.")
25. [__]   25. [__]

26. 1985 income from IRS Form 1040–line 32, 1040A–line 14, or 1040EZ–line 3 (Use the worksheet in the instructions.)
26. $ _____ .00   26. $ _____ .00

27. 1985 U.S. income tax paid (IRS Form 1040–line 50, 1040A–line 23, or 1040EZ–line 9)
27. $ _____ .00   27. $ _____ .00

28. a. 1985 deduction for a married couple when both work (IRS Form 1040–line 30 or 1040A–line 12)
28a. $ _____ .00   28a. $ _____ .00

b. 1985 payments to an IRA and/or Keogh (IRS Form 1040–total of lines 26 and 27 or 1040A–line 11)
28b. $ _____ .00   28b. XXXXXXXXXXXXX

29. 1985 itemized deductions (IRS Form 1040, Schedule A–line 24. Write in "0" if deductions were not itemized.)
29. $ _____ .00   29. $ _____ .00

30. 1985 income earned from work (See instructions.)
30a. Father $ _____ .00   30a. Student $ _____ .00
30b. Mother $ _____ .00   30b. Spouse $ _____ .00

31. 1985 untaxed income and benefits
a. Social security benefits
31a. $ _____ .00   31a. $ _____ .00
b. Aid to Families with Dependent Children (AFDC or ADC)
31b. $ _____ .00   31b. $ _____ .00
c. Other untaxed 1985 income and benefits from the worksheet in the instructions
31c. $ _____ .00   31c. $ _____ .00

32. 1985 medical and dental expenses not paid by insurance
32. $ _____ .00   32. $ _____ .00

33. 1985 elementary, junior high, and high school tuition paid (Don't include any tuition paid for the student.)
33. $ _____ .00   33. $ _____ .00

34. Expected 1986 taxable and untaxed income and benefits (See instructions.)
34. $ _____ .00

If you are filling in only the gray shaded areas, skip to Section F
Don't answer **34**, **35a, 35b, 35c**, and **36**.
XXXXXXXXXXXXX

If you are filling in the blue shaded areas, answer 35 and 36 about the student (and spouse). Don't include any financial aid such as College Work-Study earnings.

35. a. Student's (and spouse's) 1985 income from IRS Form 1040–line 32, 1040A–line 14, or 1040EZ–line 3 (See instructions.)
35a. $ _____ .00

b. Student's (and spouse's) 1985 U.S. income tax paid (IRS Form 1040–line 50, 1040A–line 23, or 1040EZ–line 9)
35b. $ _____ .00

c. Student's (and spouse's) 1985 untaxed income and benefits (See instructions.)
35c. $ _____ .00

36. Student's (and spouse's) savings and net assets (See instructions.)
36. $ _____ .00

Section F—Asset Information

	Parents — What is it worth now?	What is owed on it?	Student (and spouse) — What is it worth now?	What is owed on it?
37. Cash, savings, and checking accounts	37. $ ___ .00	XXXXXXXXXXXXX	37. $ ___ .00	XXXXXXXXXXXXX
38. Home (Renters write in "0.")	38. $ ___ .00	$ ___ .00	38. $ ___ .00	$ ___ .00
39. Other real estate and investments	39. $ ___ .00	$ ___ .00	39. $ ___ .00	$ ___ .00
40. Business and farm	40. $ ___ .00	$ ___ .00	40. $ ___ .00	$ ___ .00

Section G—Other Information and Signatures

41. List names and CSS code numbers of the colleges and programs that are to get information from this FAF. **Don't list** federal student aid programs. Be sure you enclose the right fee. See the instructions and 42 below.

Name	City and state	CSS Code No.	Housing Code*

42. Fee: Check the box next to the number of colleges and programs listed in **41**
1 ☐ $7.00   3 ☐ $18.00   5 ☐ $29.00   7 ☐ $40.00
2 ☐ $12.50   4 ☐ $23.50   6 ☐ $34.50   8 ☐ $45.50

Mail this FAF with a check or money order for the right amount made out to the College Scholarship Service. **This FAF will be returned to you if no fee is enclosed.**

43. Do you give CSS permission to send information from this FAF to the U.S. Department of Education? (Answer "Yes" if you want to be considered for the Pell Grant, Supplemental Educational Opportunity Grant, College Work-Study, National Direct Student Loan, or Guaranteed Student Loan programs.) Yes ☐ 1   No ☐ 2

44. Do you give the U.S. Department of Education permission to send family and financial information from this FAF to
a. the financial aid agency in your state? Yes ☐ 1   No ☐ 2
b. the first college (or its representative) in **41**? Yes ☐ 1   No ☐ 2
Note: Answering "Yes" to **44a** and **44b** will not meet the requirements of most states and colleges for applying for financial aid. See instructions.

45. (For office use only) [00]

*Housing Codes for 1986-87 (Enter only one code for each college.)
– Campus residence hall   3 – Parents' home   6 – Off-campus
– Campus married   4 – Relatives' home   apartment/house
student housing   5 – Off-campus residence hall   7 – Other type of housing

Certification: All of the information on this form is true and complete to the best of my knowledge. If asked by an authorized official, I agree to give proof of the information that I have given on this form. I realize that this proof may include a copy of my 1985 U.S., state, or local income tax return. I also realize that if I don't give proof when asked, the student may not get aid.

Don't complete, sign, or date before January 1, 1986.

1 _____ Student's signature
2 _____ Student's spouse's signature
3 _____ Father's signature
4 _____ Mother's signature

Write in the month and day and then check the year completed   Month   Day   Year 1 ☐ 1986   2 ☐ 1987

CONTINUE WITH QUESTION 46 ON THE NEXT PAGE. ⟶

Financial Aid Form—Side II School Year 1986-87

46. Student's name ⎣ ⎦ ⎣ ⎦ ⎣ ⎦
Last   First   M.I.

Section H—Parents' Information

47. Check one box: ☐ father ☐ stepfather ☐ other **(Explain in 66.)**
  a. Name _____
  b. Street address _____
  c. City/State/Zip _____
  d. Occupation/Title/Rank _____
  e. Employer _____
  f. Years of continuous employment with above employer ⎣ ⎦
  g. Is parent covered by this employer's pension plan? Yes ☐ 1 No ☐ 2
  h. Social security number ⎣ ⎦ — ⎣ ⎦ — ⎣ ⎦

48. Check one box: ☐ mother ☐ stepmother ☐ other **(Explain in 66.)**
  a. Name _____
  b. Street address _____
  c. City/State/Zip _____
  d. Occupation/Title/Rank _____
  e. Employer _____
  f. Years of continuous employment with above employer ⎣ ⎦
  g. Is parent covered by this employer's pension plan? Yes ☐ 1 No ☐ 2
  h. Social security number ⎣ ⎦ — ⎣ ⎦ — ⎣ ⎦

49. Breakdown of income in 26

	1985	Estimated 1986
a. Wages, salaries, tips— father or stepfather	$ .00	$ .00
b. Wages, salaries, tips— mother or stepmother	$ .00	$ .00
c. Interest income	$ .00	$ .00
d. Dividends after IRS exclusion	$ .00	$ .00
e. Net income (or loss) from business, farm, rents, royalties, partnerships, estates, trusts, etc. If a loss, enter the amount in (parentheses) **(Explain in 66.)**		
f. Other taxable income such as alimony received, capital gains (or losses), pensions, annuities, etc. **(Explain in 66.)**	$ .00	$ .00
g. Adjustments to income, including IRA/ Keogh payments and working couple deduction (Give only IRS allowable amounts. See worksheet in the instructions for 26. **Explain in 66.**)	$ .00	$ .00
h. Total (Add 49a-49f, minus 49g.) This is the answer to 26.	$ .00	$ .00

50. Monthly home mortgage or rental payment (If none, explain in 66.) $ .00

51. If parents own a home, give
  a. year purchased ⎣ 1 9 ⎦ **b.** purchase price $ .00

52. If parents included investments or other real estate in 39, list

	What is it worth now?	What is owed on it?
a. investments	$ .00	$ .00
b. other real estate	$ .00	$ .00

53. Breakdown of other untaxed income and benefits in 31c
(See instructions and the worksheet for 31c.)

Amounts from IRS tax forms		1985
a. Dividend exclusion from Form 1040, line 9b or 1040A, line 8b		$ .00
b. Untaxed portions of unemployment compensation from Form 1040, line 20a minus 20b or 1040A, line 9a minus 9b		$ .00
c. Earned income credit from Form 1040, line 59 or 1040A, line 24b		$ .00
d. Untaxed portions of pensions from Form 1040, line 17a minus 17b		$ .00
e. Credit for federal tax on special fuels from Form 1040, line 62		$ .00
f. Dividend reinvestment exclusion from Form 1040, Schedule B, line 8		$ .00
g. Foreign income exclusion from Form 2555, line 39		$ .00
h. Untaxed portions of capital gains		$ .00
i. Untaxed portions of railroad retirement benefits		$ .00
Other untaxed income		
j. Child support received		$ .00
k. Welfare benefits (except AFDC or ADC, which you should have reported in 31b)		$ .00
l. Workers' Compensation		$ .00
m. Job Training Partnership Act noneducational benefits		$ .00
n. Veterans benefits such as Death Pension Dependency and Indemnity Compensation (DIC), etc. (Don't include educational benefits or VA Vocational Rehabilitation Program benefits for postsecondary education.)		$ .00
o. Interest on tax-free bonds		$ .00
p. Housing, food, and other living allowances for military, clergy, and others (Include cash payments and cash value of benefits.)		$ .00
q. Any other untaxed income and benefits including Black Lung Benefits, etc.		$ .00
r. Total (Add 53a-53q.) This is the answer to 31c.		$ .00

54. Estimated 1986 untaxed income and benefits (Social security, Aid to Families with Dependent Children, and, as in 53 above, other untaxed income and benefits)

Estimated 1986 $ .00

55. Divorced or separated parents (To be completed by the parent who files this form)
  a. Student's natural or adoptive parents are:
    ☐ Divorced
    ☐ Legally separated
    ☐ Separated—no court action
    Date of divorce or separation ⎣ ⎦ ⎣ ⎦ Month Year
  b. Other parent's name _____
    Home address _____
    Occupation/Title/Rank _____
    Employer _____
  c. According to court order, when will support for student end? Month ⎣ ⎦ Year ⎣ ⎦

	1985	Estimated 1986
d. Amount of child support received for the student	$ .00	$ .00
e. Total amount of child support received for all children	$ .00	$ .00
f. Amount of alimony received by parent who files this form	$ .00	$ .00
g. Is there an agreement specifying a contribution for student's education? Yes ☐ No ☐ If yes, how much per year?	$ .00	$ .00

  h. Who claimed student as a tax exemption for 1985? _____
  i. If there are special circumstances, check here ☐ and explain in **66.**

Section I—Information about Family Members

56. Give information for all family members included in **23a (blue shaded area)** and **23a (gray shaded area)**. Always give the student's information on line 1. For persons not in school, give only name, age, and relationship. If there are more than seven family members, list first those persons who will be in college at least half-time and check the box at the beginning of this question. List only seven family members on the lines below. If there are more than seven, list them in **66** below.

Check this box if you don't have enough room to list all family members in this question. Use 66 below. Full name of family member	Age	Relationship to student (Use code below)	1985-86 educational information					1986-87 educational information			
			Name of school or college 1985-86 school year	Year in school or college	Tuition and fees	Room and board	Scholarships, grants, and educational loans	Parents contribution	Name of school or college 1986-87 school year	full-time or more / half-time / less than half-time (Check box if attending college)		
Student Applicant												
	·											

Use correct code: 1 - Student's parent: 2 - Student's brother or sister: 3 - Student's spouse: 4 - Student's son or daughter. 5 - Other (Explain in 66.)

Section J—Student's Information

7. Student's (and spouse's) resources (Don't enter monthly amounts.)

	Summer 1986 (3 months)	School Year 1986-87 (9 months)
a. Student's wages, salaries, tips, etc. (before taxes and deductions. Don't include work-study earnings.)	$ .00	$ .00
b. Spouse's wages, salaries, tips, etc. (before taxes and deductions. Don't include work-study earnings.)	$ .00	$ .00
c. Other taxable income (interest, dividends, etc.)	● $ .00	$ .00
d. Veterans educational benefits	$ .00	$ .00
e. Aid to Families with Dependent Children (AFDC or ADC)	$ .00	$ .00
f. Estimated cash contribution from student's parents (See instructions.)	● $ .00	$ .00
g. Grants, scholarships, fellowships, assistantships, loans, and other aid already awarded (**Explain in 66.**)	$ .00	$ .00
h. Other untaxed income and benefits (**Explain in 66.**)	$ .00	$ .00
Total resources (Add **a-h.**)	$ .00	$ .00

58. List all colleges, including city and state, that the student has attended since high school up to and including the present. If you need more space, continue in 66.

Name, city, and state of college	Period of attendance (mo./yr. to mo./yr.)	Received financial aid?	CSS Code Number
		Yes ☐ No ☐	
		Yes ☐ No ☐	
		Yes ☐ No ☐	

59. College degree or certificate student will be working toward _____

60. Student's expected date of completion of college degree or certificate ___ Month ___ Year

61. Student's
a. Occupation _____
b. Employer _____
c. Will you continue to work for this employer during the 1986-87 school year? Yes ☐ No ☐

62. Student's spouse's
a. Occupation _____
b. Employer _____
c. College in 1986-87 _____

63. Student's monthly home mortgage or rental payment, if any (If none, explain in 66.) $ .00

64. If student owns a home, give
a. year purchased 1,9,
b. purchase price $ .00

65. If student included investments or other real estate in 39, list

	What is it worth now?	What is owed on it?
a. investments	$ .00	$ .00
b. other real estate	$ .00	$ .00

Section K—Explanations/Special Circumstances

66. Use the space below to list types and amounts of income or expense for questions **49e-49g** and **57g-57h.** Also explain any unusual expenses, educational and other debts, or special circumstances (such as question **22**). If more space is needed, attach additional sheets of paper. When you are done, make a copy of the FAF for your records.

You are charged a fee for having copies of the FAF or FFS made and sent to colleges. For instance, the 1986–87 fees for having one to three copies of the FAF sent to colleges or scholarship programs are $7.00 for one copy, $12.50 for two copies, and $18.00 for three copies.

Financial need analysis shows how much you can reasonably be expected to spend a year on college expenses, but your financial need in a specific college and program is the difference between the student expense budget for that program and the amount you can afford to spend. You would have to obtain an actual student expense budget from the college itself. This information is also available in *The College Cost Book*, an annually revised publication of the College Board.

Procedures differ slightly when the Application for Federal Student Aid is used to calculate your financial need. Within four to six weeks after you send in the completed form, you will receive a Student Aid Report (SAR) giving a number called your Student Aid Index (SAI), which is the dollar amount you can be asked to contribute to college costs. It is then your responsibility to send or bring your SAR to the financial aid office. The SAI is *not* a dollar amount. The college uses its costs of attendance and the information on your Student Aid Report to determine whether you are eligible for any student aid, including Pell Grants.

In analyzing your need, the CSS, ACT, PHEAA, and DOE use elaborate systems designed to be as fair as possible to all applicants for financial aid.

Estimating Your Financial Need

Use the worksheet for self-supporting students and tables on pp. 81–82 to estimate your financial need as it might be calculated by the common methodology of the CSS, ACT, PHEAA, and DOE. Since federal aid provisions may change from year to year, your actual financial need analysis results for any given year may differ substantially from those indicated by the estimate form.

It is intended for working adult students who are self-supporting rather than financially dependent on their parents. Financial aid policies generally require that anyone applying as a self-supporting student must meet every one of the following three criteria for the preceding year, the current year, and the coming year:

1. The student has not lived in a parent's home for more than six weeks during the year.
2. The student has not been claimed as a dependent on a parent's federal income tax return.
3. The student has not received more than $750 in financial support from a parent.

Worksheet for Self-Supporting Students

Estimating What Self-Supporting Students May be Asked to Pay	Student	Denise Single student, age 21, who works part time	Edward Married graduate student, age 30, with two children
Educational Expense Budget			
1. Direct educational costs (tuition, fees, books, etc.)		$1,550	$ 5,375
2. Living allowance (Table 1)*		5,710	12,060
3. Spouse's employment allowance (allow 35% of spouse's salary to a maximum of $2,000)**		0	2,000
A. Total Educational Expense Budget (Add 1, 2, and 3)		$7,260	$19,435
Income (for 12-month period including enrollment)			
4. Your wages, salaries, tips, and other compensation		$1,845	$ 1,500
5. Spouse's wages, salaries, tips, and other compensation		0	15,000
6. Other taxable income (dividends, interest, etc.)		20	16
7. Social Security benefits		0	0
8. Veteran's Educational Benefits		0	0
9. Other untaxed (nontaxable) income and benefits		0	0
B. Total Taxable Income (add 4, 5, and 6)		$1,865	$16,516
C. Total Untaxed Income and Benefits (add 7, 8, and 9)		$ 0	$ 0
Expenses			
10. U.S. income tax you expect to pay on total in B		0	1,120
11. Social Security (FICA) tax (7.05% times each salary to a maximum of $2,792 each)		130	1,164
12. State and local taxes (enter 8% of B)		149	1,321
D. Total Expenses (add 10, 11, and 12)		$ 279	$ 3,605
Assets			
13. Home equity (total estimated market value of your home less any unpaid balance on your mortgage)		$ 0	$24,000
14. Cash, savings, and checking accounts		500	600
15. Other investments and real estate equity (current value)		0	0
16. Business or farm (your share of total value minus indebtedness, and enter the value from Table 2)		0	0
E. Total Net Assets (add 13, 14, 15, and 16)		$ 500	$24,600
Deductions			
17. Asset Protection Allowance (Table 3)		0	9,300
F. Discretionary Net Worth (subtract 17 from E)		$ 500	$15,300
Student Contribution			
18. Student contribution from taxable income (subtract D from B, use Table 4)***		$1,110	$ 9,038
19. Student contribution from untaxed income and benefits (multiply C by 100%)		0	0
20. Student contribution from assets (multiply F by 35% if unmarried or married with no children; multiply F by 12% if unmarried or married with children)		175	1,836
G. Total Student Contribution (add 18, 19, and 20)***		$1,285	$10,874
H. Student Financial Need (subtract G from A)		$5,975	$8,561

*Some institutions may not use Table 1 for determining the independent student living allowance. Check with your financial aid administrator.

**The spouse's employment allowance is optional, and not all institutions use it. Check with your financial aid administrator.

***Most institutions expect a *minimum contribution from income*, usually $1,200, from all self-supporting students. There is an additional minimum expected contribution from a spouse of $4,200, unless he or she also is a student, in which case the additional minimum is also $1,200.

Tables for Worksheet for Self-Supporting Students

Table 1. Independent student allowance (for 12 months) (Item 2)

Family size (including student)	Student's age 34 or less	Student's age 35 or more
1	$ 5,710	$ 5,870
2	7,660	10,600
3	10,110	13,200
4	12,060	16,300
5	15,300	19,230
6	18,090	22,490
Each additional	+ 1,650	+ 2,050

Table 2. Adjustment of business or farm net worth (Item 16)

Net worth (NW) of business or farm	Adjusted net worth of business or farm
Less than $1	$0
$ 1 to $ 60,000	40% of NW
$ 60,001 to 180,000	$ 24,000 plus 50% of NW over $ 60,000
$180,001 to 300,000	$ 84,000 plus 60% of NW over $180,000
$300,001 or more	$156,000 plus 100% of NW over $300,000

Table 3. Asset protection allowance (Item 17)

Student's age	Student's family size Two or more	Student's family size One
25 or less	$ 0	$ 0
26	1,900	1,400
27	3,700	2,900
28	5,600	4,300
29	7,400	5,800
30	9,300	7,200
31	11,100	8,700
32	13,000	10,100
33	14,800	11,600
34	16,700	13,000
35–39	22,200	17,400
40–44	29,100	22,700
45–49	33,500	25,600
50–54	38,700	28,900
55–59	45,900	33,100
60–64	54,900	38,500
65 or more	61,400	42,300

Table 4. Available taxable income (ATI) rates (Item 18)

Family size	Student's available income (AI)	12-month contribution from taxable income (TI)
1	$ 0 to $ 8,500	70% of AI
	8,501 or more	$ 5,950 plus 90% of AI over $ 8,500
2	$ 0 to $11,400	70% of AI
	11,401 or more	$ 7,980 plus 90% of AI over $11,400
3	$ 0 to $15,000	70% of AI
	15,001 or more	$10,500 plus 90% of AI over $15,000
4	$ 0 to $18,000	70% of AI
	18,001 or more	$12,600 plus 90% of AI over $18,000
5	$ 0 to $22,800	70% of AI
	22,801 or more	$15,960 plus 90% of AI over $22,800
6 or more	$ 0 to $26,900	70% of AI
	26,901 or more	$18,830 plus 90% of AI over $26,900

Aid applicants who do not meet these criteria are usually required to have their parents submit data so that parental income and assets can be taken into account as sources of funds for the student's college costs.

Consult These Sources in Seeking Financial Aid

College Financial Aid Offices

The college financial aid office is one of your most important sources of information and help in getting financial aid of all types, including aid sponsored by:

- the federal government
- the state government
- the local government
- various private organizations

Staff members at financial aid offices typically handle heavy work loads. To make the most effective use of their time and yours, learn as much as you can on your own from the material to which they refer you so that your questions are specific and pertinent to your needs.

Your Employer

According to the National Institute for Work and Learning, more than 92 percent of all companies having 1,000 or more employees and more than 82 percent of those with 500 to 1,000 employees have tuition-aid plans. Find out from the personnel office if your company has such a plan. These plans typically pay the tuition costs and related fees for college studies voluntarily taken by the employee outside working hours. Most are tuition-reimbursement plans, which pay back the employee's tuition and fees after the coursework is satisfactorily completed. Some are advance-payment plans. Some pay only for coursework directly related to the employee's present job. Others pay for any recognized educational courses, while still others may also pay for the costs of books and supplies.

If you happen to be looking for a new job, consider working for an employer with a tuition-aid plan. Some adults choose to work for a college or university to get the 6 credits or more of tuition-free courses offered college staff members as an employee benefit. You may find it helpful in checking on such tuition-aid programs to consult *Corporate Tuition Aid Programs: A Directory of College Financial Aid for Employees at America's Largest Corporations*, by Joseph P. O'Neill.

Federal Student Aid Programs

Most colleges and state agencies routinely require applicants to apply for federal aid, including Pell Grants, as part of the overall financial aid application process. You can apply by checking the appropriate box on an FAF, SAAC, FFS, or PHEAA application, or by completing the AFSA. All forms are available from the colleges. To receive an annually revised information booklet, *The Student Guide: Five Federal Financial Aid Programs*, write to:

Federal Student Aid Programs
Department DEA-86
Pueblo, CO 81009

You may also be able to get copies of the AFSA and the booklet from college financial aid offices, public libraries, and post offices.

The five federal programs are Pell Grants, Guaranteed Student Loans, and three programs available only through college financial aid offices— Supplemental Educational Opportunity Grants (SEOG), College Work-Study (CWS), and National Direct Student Loans (NDSL).

Public Libraries

Both the local branch public library and the larger main library are good sources of financial aid information. Ask the reference librarian for such information, including data on any programs especially helpful to adults.

Libraries and college financial aid offices frequently post announcements or listings of aid programs that are particularly designed for adults. The following are examples of the kinds of programs you might learn about.

Aid for Part-Time Study (APTS) Program of New York State. In the spring of 1984 New York State launched a pioneering program to provide tuition aid to part-time undergraduate students enrolled in degree programs at colleges in the state for course loads of 6 to 11 credits per semester (or 4 to 8 credits per quarter). Grants applicable only toward tuition costs range up to $2,000.

Eligibility requirements include completion of at least 6 semester-hour credits and New York State net taxable income (as defined for state income tax returns) of $15,000 or less for an independent (self-supporting) student.

Clairol Loving Care Scholarship Program. A unique scholarship program open only to women over age 30 who are studying for a career in an accredited program is sponsored by the Clairol beauty aids firm. Starting in

1985, its eleventh year of operation, this scholarship program increased its total annual aid to $75,000. Scholarships range up to $1,000.

Information and applications are available by sending a stamped, self-addressed envelope to the Clairol Scholarship Program, care of Business and Professional Women's Foundation, 2012 Massachusetts Avenue NW, Washington, DC 20036.

Also available through the program is a folder, "Educational Financial Aid Sources for Women," sent without charge on request to the Educational Financial Aid Sources for Women, Box 14680, Baltimore, MD 21268.

Membership Organizations

If you are a member of an organization such as a church or synagogue, a civic or community organization, a lodge or fraternal organization, a labor union, or a veterans' society like the American Legion, find out if that organization sponsors a scholarship program. Most programs of this sort are for the children of members of the organizations, but in some cases they offer awards to members themselves.

Professional Societies

Write to any professional society that accredits college programs in your career area to request information about financial aid for study in the field. Organizations of this kind often have college aid listings.

6. Securing Admission and Financial Aid

Applying for college admission and financial aid can involve much paperwork and many unfamiliar tests. This chapter tells how to carry out the application process with the least strain and the best results.

Identify All Application Requirements and Deadlines

One of the first steps to simplify the process of applying is to organize your overall campaign. Many colleges and aid programs have much the same requirements. By making a master plan to meet the requirements for all applications insofar as possible, you eliminate duplicated effort and needless expense.

At the outset, then, for every college and program you want to try, collect the current, complete, official instructions on applying for admission, financial aid, or both. Applying to two or three colleges is advisable if they are equally appropriate and if there is any question of not being admitted to one. One factor to consider is the admissions application fee costs of from $10 to $25 per college, unless you request hardship waivers. Applying to only one college, however, is perfectly all right if that college represents a workable choice and is virtually your only available opportunity.

Compile Your Master List

With all the official instructions for applying at hand, compile your master application requirements and deadlines list. Use Worksheet 8 to note the items required and the submission deadlines for every application you will make.

Filling out this master schedule will help you see how making one request to have high school transcripts sent—or taking one college entrance test or writing one basic essay or completing one financial aid form—can meet the requirements of a number of colleges and aid programs. Even filling out one admissions application form assembles in convenient array many of the facts you'll need for all other application forms.

Post Your Projected Action Dates on a Calendar

Using your master list, consolidate the actions you will take to meet application requirements. On a pocket or desk calendar that you refer to daily, post on the appropriate dates each action you should take to meet your admissions requirements.

Your calendar should show, for example, not only the deadline date by which a college must have your score on a required test like the Scholastic Aptitude Test (SAT), but also the date by which you must register for the test. You should also record the date on which you will take the test and where you'll take it. You might also want to enter a reminder to get a book of sample tests with which to practice, and the date to start working questions on the sample tests.

Make a check on your calendar each time a task is accomplished. This record will show what actions you have taken and which remain to be carried out.

Keep Orderly Files

Set up a simple file system to keep track of all the paperwork that results from your applications. Start with the statements of requirements, application instructions, and information bulletins or catalogs that are your original source material.

Then, make and file copies of all your application documents, registrations, letters, notes (including those made during conferences by phone or in person), and notices or replies received. Having copies of everything you send can save you hours of duplicated labor if something you've supplied gets lost. Documents can get misdirected in the mail or lost or misplaced in handling.

WORKSHEET 8. MASTER APPLICATION REQUIREMENTS AND DEADLINES LIST

Application to Which College or Financial Aid Program

Item				

1. Admissions application form   Required ☐   Required ☐   Required ☐   Required ☐

Deadline date   _____   _____   _____   _____

Essay   Required ☐   Required ☐   Required ☐   Required ☐

2. Financial aid application form   Required ☐   Required ☐   Required ☐   Required ☐

Deadline date   _____   _____   _____   _____

3. High school transcript or equivalency-diploma   Required ☐   Required ☐   Required ☐   Required ☐

Deadline date   _____   _____   _____   _____

4. College transcript   Required ☐   Required ☐   Required ☐   Required ☐

Deadline date   _____   _____   _____   _____

5. Test scores

SAT   Required ☐   Required ☐   Required ☐   Required ☐

ACT   Required ☐   Required ☐   Required ☐   Required ☐

Other:

_____   Required ☐   Required ☐   Required ☐   Required ☐

Deadline date   _____   _____   _____   _____

WORKSHEET 8. MASTER APPLICATION REQUIREMENTS AND DEADLINES LIST

Application to Which College or Financial Aid Program

Item				
6. Recommendation letters				
(1) _____	Required ☐	Required ☐	Required ☐	Required ☐
(2) _____	Required ☐	Required ☐	Required ☐	Required ☐
(3) _____	Required ☐	Required ☐	Required ☐	Required ☐
Deadline date				
7. Interview	Required ☐	Required ☐	Required ☐	Required ☐
Deadline date				
8. Other:				
_____	Required ☐	Required ☐	Required ☐	Required ☐
_____	Required ☐	Required ☐	Required ☐	Required ☐
_____	Required ☐	Required ☐	Required ☐	Required ☐
_____	Required ☐	Required ☐	Required ☐	Required ☐
Deadline date				

Notes:

Conveniently filed copies are also useful to refer to in making additional applications, or in answering questions or requests you get in response to your application materials.

Providing Required Application Items

Application Forms

Complete your application forms as legibly and neatly as possible, preferably using a typewriter. Use the same legibility and care in preparing all your application documents and letters. Doing so conveys a favorable impression of yourself as a capable, effective person. It also avoids outright errors in deciphering facts about yourself or even functional details like your mailing address.

If you've decided to seek financial aid, make sure that you apply for both admission and financial aid. Applying for admission does not automatically mean you are applying for financial aid. Follow each college's instructions for financial aid applicants precisely. These may or may not require a separate aid application form, and they often call for extra information and earlier deadline dates than those required for persons applying only for admission.

Application Essays

The applicant is sometimes required to write an essay to submit with the application form. A typical subject is the applicant's goals or purposes if admitted to the program.

Essays of this kind need not be long; several paragraphs are usually enough. Be honest and candid in an application essay. Don't exaggerate or dramatize. Most important, try to make your writing as clear and correct as possible. Clarity and correct English are two qualities especially looked for in such essays. If you are uncertain about spelling and grammar, consult a dictionary whenever necessary and have someone knowledgeable in writing go over the essay with you. Then, after revising and correcting the draft, make a clean, clear copy to submit. Even professional authors (including the author of this book) typically revise and correct their work in one or more drafts before the final version.

High School Transcripts or Equivalency Diplomas

You don't need to be a high school graduate to enter certain college programs. How you can make up for not having a high school diploma will be explained shortly.

For an admissions applicant who did finish high school, however, colleges commonly require a certified high school record reporting the courses taken and grades earned by the applicant (possibly with other information, such as the student's grade point average, rank in graduating class, and scores on selected tests).

Such an official record of all courses and grades in an entire program of study and the award of a diploma or other completion credential is called a transcript.

You can meet a college's requirement for your high school transcript by writing to the high school from which you graduated (or its school district office), identifying yourself and your high school and years of attendance and graduation, and requesting that a copy of your transcript be sent to the college's admissions office.

You may make such a request even if you graduated as long as 40 or 50 years earlier. Student records are often kept permanently. Make your request four to eight months in advance, though, if you have been out of school for a number of years. Otherwise, make the request for your high school transcript at least six to eight weeks before a college's deadline. In making any high school requests, remember that the school may be completely closed from mid-June to mid-September.

Ask the school or school system to send a transcript copy to each college requiring one, and give the complete, correct address for each. Schools often send transcripts without charge, but your school may be one that makes a nominal charge for this service. To be acceptable to admissions offices, transcripts must be sent directly from the school to the college (inasmuch as a copy coming from an applicant might have been forged).

If you earned a high school equivalency diploma, have the adult education program or other agency that awarded the equivalency diploma send a transcript of your records to the college admissions offices.

If your high school records have somehow been destroyed through fire or other accident, ask the college admissions offices for instructions on how to proceed. Affidavits of specified kinds attesting to your high school graduation may be accepted.

If You Don't Have a High School Diploma

Some colleges permit an applicant without a high school diploma to take courses on a trial basis. The terms of that trial should provide for having the diploma requirement waived—or being granted an equivalency diploma—based on the satisfactory completion of a specified minimum number of credits, like 24. If possible, such coursework should be fully acceptable in the study program leading to the degree you want.

As an alternative, you could study for and take tests to earn your high school equivalency diploma. Preparatory classes and testing for equivalency diplomas are regularly offered by public high school systems. You can find out how to earn your equivalency diploma by writing or telephoning the office of the superintendent of schools of your community public school system. The information is probably also available in a public library.

College Transcripts

Transcripts of previous college studies you've completed are also often required for admission. You can request these in the same way you did your high school transcript.

Your college transcripts can be especially valuable to you. Such transcripts provide the basis for awarding you "transfer credit" toward your degree, if your previous college courses are acceptable in content and difficulty level for your degree program.

Test Scores

Many college programs designed especially for adults have no test requirements. For others, though, you might have to take an entrance test. The entrance tests most often required for undergraduate admission are the Scholastic Aptitude Test (SAT) of the College Board and the American College Testing Program Assessment (ACT).

Individual colleges set their requirements for these tests. A number of colleges accept the results of either the SAT or ACT. Others require one or the other, so check with the college of your choice before registering for either test.

These tests are given several times during the year on Saturday (or on an alternate test day for those whose religious beliefs preclude Saturday testing) at schools and test centers throughout the country. College admissions instructions will specify the latest date by which to take the test.

Information about the tests, test registration, fees, and testing sites is available from the following locations:

The College Board
Admissions Testing Program
Box 592
Princeton, NJ 08541

ACT Registration
Box 414
Iowa City, IA 52234

Study materials with which to prepare for these tests are provided in the bulletins and other literature sent when you register. You should not need any other help in preparing for the tests.

Relax in preparing for and taking the SAT, ACT, or any other entrance tests required. With adult students, colleges often use test results for guidance in the right selection of courses and for placement rather than for admissions acceptance or rejection.

Some colleges require other tests such as the Achievement Tests of the College Board, which are tests in specific high school subjects (like chemistry, French, or American history). If a college requires these or other tests, it will give you the necessary information.

Recommendation Letters

Colleges commonly require a secondary school recommendation for admissions applicants who are high school graduates. If the college you're applying to requires a school recommendation, request it at the time you write for your high school transcript. Since you may no longer have any personal contacts at the school, ask if the guidance department can write a recommendation based on an interpretation of your transcript, using it to evaluate your capability for academic work on the college level. Add information about your work or courses you have taken that may be relevant.

If other recommendation letters are required, request them from present or former teachers, from supervisors at work, or from professionals who have some acquaintance with your capabilities for college studies. Ask for these evaluations long before the deadline so that the persons involved have ample time to draft their statements.

Interviews

Schedule required interviews well before the deadline specified. An admissions interview gives you the opportunity to get firsthand information about the college and its programs. Don't be nervous about interviews; they rarely influence admissions decisions, especially in the case of adult student applicants.

How to Handle Offers of Admission and Financial Aid

Several weeks or even months may go by before you start to receive decisions on your admissions and financial aid applications.

If you've applied to more than one college, try to wait until you've heard from all the colleges before deciding which offer to accept. Should you be required to make a decision on one college's offer before you know whether you've been accepted elsewhere, either try to get an extension on replying to the first offer, or ask for an early decision on your other applications.

Once you have thoughtfully considered your options and made your decision, send a gracious acceptance letter by the reply deadline. Be sure to respond to any other acceptances you receive, declining the offer and expressing gratitude for the consideration you have received. This sort of courtesy is a good basic policy and might even have some practical value to you at a later time.

7. Getting Off to a Good Start: Course Selection, Registration, and Opening Classes

Adult students often feel uncertain or even fearful about starting off in college. It's a realistic concern because a good start can have a substantial effect on how well you do in your studies overall, but you needn't feel anxious if you do some thoughtful planning. This chapter will guide you through the pivotal activities of choosing courses, registering, and beginning classes.

Registration

Registration is the first major activity following your admission to college. It is then that you plan how many and which courses you'll take, with which professors or instructors (to the extent you can choose), and what the schedule of your classes and your daily life will be for the coming months.

It's also the time that you may have to make split-second last-minute decisions on changes of courses, professors, or schedules, and it's the time you pay tuition and fees for the coming term.

The main steps in preparing for and completing registration effectively are as follows.

Locate and Meet with Good Advisers

All other steps in your initial registration go more smoothly if you have one or more good counselors to advise you whenever major decisions come up.

Ideally, you'll be assigned to a good basic adviser by the college. But if you're not assigned an adviser, or if the adviser you are assigned seems uninterested or uninformed, look for others.

If you're unsure where to start, consult with the admissions office. Another possibility is to ask for advice from the head of the study program you've chosen or the head of the department in which you plan to major. The faculty member serving as head (or that person's secretary) either will be able to help you or will refer you to someone else who can. Senior students in your study program may act as advisers.

Once you locate the most understanding and best-informed advisers you can find, talk over your study plans and questions with them. Their ideas and suggestions can help a great deal.

Planning Your Course Selections and Schedule

Make sure to start the job of planning courses, course sections, and class schedule at least several days before the scheduled opening of your registration period for the term. Regular registration normally runs for several days before the beginning of classes.

For the planning task you need the college's catalog or other bulletin of detailed course descriptions for the coming term—material that gives such facts as:

- official course numbers and names
- brief summaries of course content
- credit value of the course
- days of the week and hours of the day when the course sessions are held
- room number and building where the course sessions are held
- prerequisite courses (required or recommended to be taken before enrolling in the course being described)
- name(s) of the faculty member(s) teaching the course

Luckily, colleges often give catalog listings of typical course combinations recommended for students in each level of a program. Start your planning with such a listing, if available. Under any circumstances, build your first-term schedule around your program's introductory courses and basic requirements. With these you might include one elective course that fits your program objectives and study interests.

Draft several different possible combinations of courses for your first term. Tentatively decide which courses you might add or drop from your draft schedules if you choose a lighter or heavier course load. Bring your draft schedules with you when you go for a planning conference with your adviser. That will prepare you to take the fullest advantage of the adviser's suggestions on selecting courses and instructors, scheduling course sequences, and completing requirements. Choose some possible substitutions of courses or hours to fall back on in case you can't get precisely the selection and schedule you want.

Coping with the Registration Maze

Steel yourself for delays in long lines, for confusion, and for much paperwork and red tape in the process of registration itself. They typify registration at almost any college.

Go to the designated location at the earliest time you can manage in the registration period—if possible, on the very first day or night of the registration period. By going early you can avoid being closed out of desired courses and sections because of full enrollments.

Be as alert, resourceful, and patient as you can during registration. Get all the details involved as correct and as close to what you want as possible. Stay calm about closings of courses, errors in listings, or other last-minute changes that affect your plans. If you run into difficulties or problems, consult with advisers who are present at registration sessions to provide help.

The end result is your program for the coming term, and that is not irrevocable. There is usually a period running for several days after registration in which changes in courses and class sessions can be made without penalty. There is also a specified time after the opening of classes during which students can drop courses for which they have registered, with full or partial refunds of their tuition payments. For instance, a college's policy may specify a full tuition refund if the course is dropped during the first week of the term, a 75 percent refund if dropped during the second week, a 50 percent refund if dropped during the third week, and no refund if dropped thereafter.

Paying Your College Bills

One of your last steps in registration is to pay your fees and tuition for the courses in which you have registered. Come prepared with a check or cash. A number of colleges today also accept payment by major credit card.

Colleges also offer plans for installment payments of your bills for tuition and fees. Look into the terms of the school's installment plan in advance, however, because the interest rate may be higher than interest on a personal loan from a bank.

Getting Your Student ID Card

With a receipt for payment of your first-term college bills you are usually issued a student ID (identification) card that carries a color photograph of your face. The card also gives your student number, which is usually your

Social Security number. Your ID card can be as valuable as a credit card. Protect it carefully, for you will probably use it repeatedly for access to various college facilities and for student discounts.

When you've completed registration for your first term in college, consider that you've done very well if you've gotten only part of what you wanted. This first registration experience is the hardest and the strangest. Later registrations will be much easier because you'll know so much more about the systems, courses, and teachers and will have located many good sources of advice.

Many colleges offer enrolled students the opportunity to preregister. This service is usually computerized and simply requires that you submit your course request forms for the coming term before the close of your current term. It greatly simplifies the registration process.

Starting Your Coursework

Once you're registered, focus on preparing to do well in your courses. Start by outfitting yourself with basic learning tools that include the following:

- A standard desk dictionary, preferably the latest edition. Ask a teacher or librarian to recommend one if you're unsure which to choose among the many available ones.
- A manual of correct English usage. If you're taking a required introductory course in English composition, wait to see which usage reference is recommended for the course.
- A typewriter, which is highly desirable for preparing final copies of research papers or compositions.

A pocket calculator or even a microcomputer can be an essential tool for programs heavy in mathematics, science, or technology. You might wait to see what types are recommended for use in the specific program you're taking. Moreover, the college may make preferred calculators or computers available at substantial discounts. Equip yourself, too, with notebooks, pens, and a bookbag or briefcase.

The first session in each of your courses will be especially interesting, for you'll be meeting the person who teaches the course and learning essentially what the course will be like. Follow these basic steps at your first class meetings:

- Make a list of the required texts or other books to get.
- Note any special supplies or equipment that may be needed or recommended.

- If appropriate, get a reading list for the course that identifies all required textbooks and supplementary reading sources. The reading list may include the dates by which to complete specified readings.
- Get a copy of the syllabus or outline of topics covered in the course, or make notes on the instructor's verbal description of course content and coverage.
- Note the instructor's stated policies concerning attendance requirements; class participation; amount and kinds of outside assignments; numbers, kinds, and timing of term papers and exams; and basis for grading.
- Make a record of office hours when the instructor is available to answer questions or help clear up difficulties you may be having with the course.
- Ask questions about any aspect of the course that isn't clear to you, either during or after the class session.

Getting Your Textbooks and Special Supplies

Follow instructions precisely in getting the recommended textbooks and special supplies or equipment needed for your courses. A college's own bookstore or other nearby bookstores may offer used textbooks at about half the price of new copies. These could help you economize, but be sure they are the editions specified for your course and not earlier editions. Another economy is to buy new copies and sell them when you've completed the course.

Get your textbooks as soon as you know what they are, so you can start studying immediately. Initial textbook supplies sometimes sell out early in a term, and by delaying, you may have to wait until a new shipment arrives.

Begin Assignments Immediately

Get started on your assignments as soon as possible. Finishing assigned work on time is one of the best ways to succeed in your classes. Try to complete assigned readings, problems, or papers early; do not postpone assignments if you can possibly avoid it.

Of course, you can't do all your assignments at once. Schedule time slots for them and for your other responsibilities. How to manage your time is explained in chapter 10. Helpful study skills enabling you to use your time more efficiently are described in chapter 9. But starting right in on assignments with dispatch can go far to help get them done on time.

Finding Out about Library Resources and Hours

Your instructor will probably advise you whether collateral books or references for your coursework have been put on reserve in the college library.

The instructor can also tell you of any other library materials you might need to use for the course.

Investigate the suggested library resources and get acquainted generally with the library's reference room, card catalog, circulation system, and other facilities. You may find the library an ideal place in which to study.

Find out in particular what hours the library is open. Colleges with large enrollments of adult students are often open until 11 or 12 on weeknights and through long weekend hours, especially during examination periods.

Relating to Your Professors and Instructors

Try to put your relations with the professors and instructors who teach your courses on a friendly, yet essentially neutral, professional basis. In your reactions, think of them as professionals working to help you. Try to break clear of old attitudes of special awe or resentment toward teachers that may carry over from your teenage years.

Work to meet the demands they make in their courses as well as you can. If you find one of them arbitrary or mistaken at times, don't let it upset you. Professors can be wrong, just like anyone else. Most of them are essentially fair, reasonable, and considerate. Some of them are superbly inspiring. Make sure to use their help. Be careful not to fall behind in your assignments. Ask your teacher for help as soon as you find yourself in any difficulty. This will enable you to catch up before you've fallen seriously behind. It may also identify some deficiency that needs extensive remedial work.

Problems aren't the only reasons to talk with your professor. If you're doing well in a course, you may want to discuss points about it that especially interest you. Sharing interests and enthusiasm in your studies with your professors represents one of the main satisfactions and benefits of college study.

Reiating to Other Students

Fellow students are another source of help and stimulation. Among them you may find some wonderful companions and friends. At the start, you may want to be somewhat reserved with other students until you establish a solid foundation in your academic work. One thing you don't want to do is become distracted by the college's social life through new friendships. Maintain a balance between the rewards of friendship and the demands of academic work.

8. Making Adjustments at Work and at Home

For success in college while working, you'll probably need to make adjustments in two major areas—your work life and your personal life.

Work Life

The burden of degree-credit coursework can be entirely manageable if you organize your employment responsibilities to allow for your study demands. Taking the following steps in your work will help to assure success in your studies.

Avoid Severe Time Conflicts

Face the fact that working overtime on your job may be out of the question once you start college studies. Attending classes, studying, and completing assignments take 30 or more hours a week for a modest, 8-to-10-credit program. Your job, your studies, or both will suffer if you try to maintain an unrealistically heavy work schedule. Therefore, as you start off in your studies, alert your employer to the fact that during the college term you won't be able to take on overtime work. Employers are usually willing to make such adjustments for conscientious employees. Make it clear that you're concerned with maintaining the quality of your work as well as your studies and that you see both as a present and future value to the employer.

Enlist Support from Your Superiors

Let your immediate supervisor know as early as you can that you're thinking of going for your college degree. Then, when your plans are definite, arrange a meeting with your supervisor to explain your study plan and the commitments of time and effort it will take. Assure the supervisor that you will continue to give your job your very best efforts during regular working hours. But point out that you intend to give your studies your best possible effort outside working hours. You need not make any long explanations, but be sure to be clear. Ask to have your college plans reported to higher-level executives in your area and added to your personnel records. After the meeting, confirm all the points you've covered in a memo to your supervisor.

Should your employer offer a tuition-aid plan, consult your supervisor about arranging for such aid. Applying for tuition aid will probably give you some personal contact with personnel officers and bring you to the attention of higher-level managers who approve requests for aid, which could be advantageous to you.

Win Cooperation from Your Co-workers

Let your close colleagues know about your college plans as they become definite. Your aim in keeping them informed is to assure their cooperation and friendship, since you may need their help from time to time. At some point you may want to trade lunch hours, work shifts, or discretionary days off with one of them in order to finish a term paper or to study for a final exam. Enlisting their cooperation in advance can head off any problems that might otherwise develop.

Explore Possible Promotion Routes

Completing your college-degree program may qualify you for promotions with your present employer. Find out about such possibilities in your initial discussions with your supervisor, who should be able to tell you how to apply for promotion at the appropriate time.

In addition, meet with a personnel officer to discuss possible promotion opportunities. Try to do this as early as possible because the information may influence the kind of study program you decide to pursue. Keep in touch with the personnel department about possible options in your study program that may affect advancement routes. And be sure to let them know when you're within a few months of receiving your degree.

Personal Life

Making the appropriate adjustments in your personal life will help you to achieve success in your studies. Here are some suggestions.

Win Support from Those You Live With

It's very important to have the enthusiastic cooperation of the people you live with. If they resent or feel threatened by your college plans, your home life will be stressful. How to go about winning their support depends on your living situation.

Couples without children. Involve your partner as much as possible in your own developing interest in getting your college degree. Sharing your enthusiasm will help the other person prepare with you for the changes your studies will bring in your life together.

Couples with children. If you have children, they, too, need to be taken into your confidence as you make your college plans. The children will have a better understanding of what you're about if they go to school themselves.

Work out necessary child-care arrangements long in advance. Child care for which you pay becomes an added college cost to take into account. Child-care services are available at many colleges today, so look into that possibility as well as community and private facilities. Reassure your children that the changes in your family's normal routine are not going to alter your relationship or jeopardize their security.

Single parents. If you're a single parent planning on college, you'll probably want to make special efforts to win the understanding and help of your children and to reassure them that your involvement with school in no way diminishes your love for them. Even young ones are likely to cooperate if you give them a sense of how important it is to you and to them for you to do well in your studies. For instance, one divorced mother of four who earned a degree through the Regents Colleges Degree Program commented:

> Over the past three years our lives have changed considerably. . . . However, we feel we have "made it" to some extent, and that the degree belongs not only to me, but more especially to four small children who "dug in" and helped make all this successful.

Allocate Time for Home Chores

One of the major practical adjustments you may need to make concerns the amount of time you spend on home chores once you start your studies. Decide which chores are absolutely essential to maintaining a comfortable, efficient home and eliminate all extraneous activities. Consolidate shopping and various errands into one or two well-planned trips a week instead of doing them daily. Substitute nutritious one-dish meals for elaborate cooking and baking. Put off any cleaning and repair jobs that aren't an immediate necessity until you have a break between semesters. If there are other people in your household, enlist their cooperation in getting chores done. Most important, keep your homemaking responsibilities in perspective—they're only a part of your life and not necessarily the most important part while you're striving to make the grade in college.

Adjust Your Social and Recreational Life

The time pressures of college also mean major changes in your social and recreational life. You'll have less time to spend with friends, less time for sports activities and entertainment such as movies, concerts, or parties. Nevertheless, relaxation is important, so plan your recreational time as carefully as you plan your study and work time. Try to compensate in quality what you give up in quantity. And keep in mind that college itself offers new social and recreational activities related to your studies that you and your family members can enjoy.

Adjust to Having Less Money

College expenses can cut heavily into the money you have available for your personal life. One way to adjust to that is to shift as much as possible from activities that cost money to ones that are low-cost or free. Postpone expensive vacations and major purchases. View college as an adventure and an investment, with returns in present satisfactions and future income prospects from which you and your family can all benefit.

9. Building Study Skills for Confidence and Good Grades

If you've been away from high school or college for a number of years, you may feel rusty and unsure about being able to study effectively. Rather than worry about it, be sure to develop or refresh your study skills as you head into your degree program. Knowing how to study effectively virtually assures good grades and replaces anxiety with confidence.

This chapter gives you guidelines for brushing up on basic study skills. If you think you need more help, consult the list of books at the end of this chapter. You may also want to find out if your college has a learning skills development center. Such a center can give you extensive personalized help in developing your study skills as well as your skills in basic English and mathematics. Many colleges provide such centers or services today.

Boost Your Reading Speed and Comprehension

For the intensive reading required in college, you need to focus on the following skills:

1. vocabulary building
2. preliminary survey
3. concentration on content
4. eye-movement patterns

First, for vocabulary building, get in the habit of learning the meaning of new terms and words you come across in your studies. To build your vocabulary, write down any word or term you don't know when you come upon it, look it up in a dictionary, and write down its meaning. Then memorize it, using the technique explained later in the chapter. Start using the word or term in your discussions and written assignments to make it more familiar to you. To get the most from your assigned readings, look over the section or chapter in advance to identify any unfamiliar words. Write them down and look them up before your start reading. Then you'll have immediate comprehension of the text when you do read it.

Second, learn to make a preliminary survey of any reading you do. Look at the title, the headings, the first sentence, the last sentence, and the first and last sentences of each paragraph. Examine diagrams, graphs, other illustrations, and captions.

In particular, phrase a question suggested by the title and headings that your reading can answer. For instance, suppose you're assigned to read a chapter in American history on the opening of the Civil War. Your question might be, "What were the immediate causes of the war?" Phrasing a question like this will help focus your attention on the reading.

Third, concentrate while you read. Don't let your mind wander. For instance, keep that question you framed in mind and watch for the answers as you read. Stop whenever your attention falters, and put the reading aside briefly. Stretch. Take a deep breath. Get a drink of water. Then resume with complete concentration.

To aid concentration and later review, many students find it helpful to underline the main ideas and the key facts and phrases. By all means do so if it helps your concentration and recall. Marking important points in a book can help to fix them in your mind. It also makes the book a useful study guide when you're preparing for an exam. Concentration is one of the most important elements in increasing your reading speed and your recall of the facts and ideas you've read.

Fourth, using efficient eye-movement patterns can greatly increase your reading speed and comprehension. Many students read by focusing on one word at a time. But the mind soaks up meaning much faster than that and daydreams while the eye drags behind. Experts on the process of reading recommend that you shift instead to two eye fixations, or points of focus, per line of words to be read. Focus toward the left side of a line, then toward the right side of the line (at about the one-quarter point and the three-quarter point in each line). You'll find that your mind instantly absorbs the meaning of the entire phrase on each half-line your eye takes in at a single glance.

Try it first by putting your finger under each line to guide your eye focus:

one-quarter, three-quarter; one-quarter, three-quarter; and so on. Then try speeding up the movement of your finger. And finally try it just by sweeping your eye across each line. For narrow columns like those in newspapers or weekly newsmagazines, you can sweep your eye right down the middle of the column to absorb the meaning of each whole line at a glance.

Adapt your reading to the kind of material at hand and your purpose in reading. You can read a novel assigned for a literature class at high speed to grasp the story line, or at a slower pace if you're analyzing the style. But you may have to pore over a mathematics, physics, or chemistry textbook very slowly, sometimes analyzing word by word or phrase by phrase to comprehend the technical information.

A college learning skills center can help you develop these and other techniques to improve your reading.

Outline to Organize Note Taking and Plan Term Papers

Outlining is another important technique to use in studying and writing. It's a method for summarizing the structure and main points and facts of a body of information such as a textbook chapter or a class lecture. It's also vital for organizing the research and writing for your papers.

A statement of thought isn't just a series of observations. Rather, it begins with a topic or subject set forth in terms of main ideas. Each main idea is supported by related ideas or facts, which in turn are supported by subordinate ideas or facts, all of which are summed up in a conclusion.

You can recognize each of these parts from the way a professor introduces the subject of a lecture. For instance, "This morning we will consider the phenomenon of gravity." [Subject] "The three most important principles to understand in connection with gravity are these." [Main ideas]

A generalized outline would look like this, with indentions to show successive degrees of subordination.

Topic or Subject

A. Main ideas summarized
   1. First main idea identified
   2. Second main idea identified
   3. Third main idea identified
B. First main idea discussed
   1. First aspect of this main idea
      a. Fact one about this aspect
      b. Fact two about this aspect
      c. Fact three about this aspect

> 2. Second aspect of this main idea
>
> C. Second main idea discussed
>
> 1. First aspect of this main idea, etc.

Practice outlining to get the knack for doing it. Don't worry about getting an outline "just right." An outline is to help you organize your writing, summarizing, memorizing, reviewing, understanding, and learning. Use whatever kind of outline works best for you, revising and modifying it as needed.

Note Taking for Reading Assignments and Class Sessions

Outlining a reading assignment is an excellent way to help you understand and remember the key elements of what you have read. And outlining is equally useful for taking notes in class lectures and discussions. The outline helps you to review the material after class and to prepare for examinations. Information your professors write on the chalkboard as they lecture is likely to be significant, so it's wise to copy that information in your class notes.

Techniques for Memorizing

Rote memorizing isn't a particularly high-level study skill for college, but it's certainly a basic one that you use all the time. Certain techniques or devices make it easier than expending sheer brute effort. Here are some of the handiest ones.

Using an Acronym or an Acrostic

To remember a group of otherwise miscellaneous terms or names, try to put their initial letters together to form an acronym (a word or term made up of the initial letters of other words, like UNESCO for United Nations Educational, Scientific, and Cultural Organization).

For example, suppose you want to remember the names of the Great Lakes. Using the acronym HOMES brings them readily to mind: Huron, Ontario, Michigan, Erie, and Superior.

A similar memory-jogging device is the acrostic—a sentence you make up in which the first letter of each word stands for the things you want to memorize. Say that you need to memorize the first five presidents of the United States. To do so, you make up an acrostic, "Will A Jogger Madden Monday?" to remind you that the five in order were Washington, Adams, Jefferson, Madison, and Monroe. A nonsense sentence seems to result in better recall than one that makes sense.

Using Association Chains of Absurd Images

Nonsensical associations in the form of images can also be used as a memory aid. Suppose you want to remember the titles of four novels by Ernest Hemingway, and in this order: *The Sun Also Rises, A Farewell to Arms, For Whom the Bell Tolls,* and *The Old Man and the Sea.*

Imagine, then, that you are viewing a scene featuring a sunrise with the moon already risen in the sky. In the foreground is a train platform with people on it waving goodbye to a trainload of guns. Beside the track is a church topped by a steeple in which a large bell loudly clangs. Listening to the bell a short distance away is the man for whom it rings—an old man with a long white beard, who in turn stands knee-deep in the sea.

Odd as it may at first seem, that nonsensical picture should make those book titles almost unforgettable for you. Try it and see.

Standard Memorization Techniques

In addition to these and other special memorization techniques, you should know and use the standard, traditional methods. One is to break up a large body of text or a series of numbers into small chunks that you commit to memory piece by piece. For instance, you don't memorize the phone number for the admissions office at the University of California at Berkeley as 4156420200, but as 415-642-0200.

A second standard method is to write what you want to memorize, saying it as you write, and to do this over and over and over, testing your memory periodically and repeating the process until you've got it down pat. Some persons seem to have better eye memory (recalling best the visual image of written words or numbers), while others have better ear memory (recalling best what they hear). The memorization system you find most effective will depend on whether you tend to be an eye-memory or an ear-memory person.

Still a third standard memory technique is to use flash cards—small file cards on which you write anything you want to memorize (like new words, with the word on the front of the card and the definition on the back). Then you look at and say aloud what's on each card as you flip through the stack repeatedly.

How to Prepare for and Take Examinations

Doing well on examinations depends almost as much on knowledge of the study skills involved in preparing for and taking tests effectively as on mastery of the subject being tested. Here are some important general techniques to use for quizzes and examinations.

First, to prepare for a test, keep current in your coursework. Read through your notes daily. When the instructor announces a test, ask or deduce as well as you can what it will cover and what kinds of questions will be asked.

Review the pertinent parts of your notes, textbook, and any related reading assignments to be certain you understand the material and to freshen it in your memory. If the test will involve solving problems in mathematics or science, practice working a few problems of each kind you expect on the test.

When you take the test, look over all the questions at the outset and allocate your time for answering each question.

Begin by answering the easiest questions first, then the next easiest, and the hardest questions last. Doing the questions in this order is effective because it bolsters your confidence, lets you demonstrate what you do know, and often stimulates your recall of answers to the harder questions.

Make an effort to answer all the questions if you can and if time permits. Give a partial answer if you recall some but not all the material that you think the answer should contain. Respond with material you do know that has some bearing on a question even though it may not be precisely what's asked for.

Work swiftly but with care. Check your answers over if you have time to do so near the end of the test session, to repair any possible slips or omissions. Then, when you are done, forget the examination completely until you learn the results. From those results learn all you can to do still better the next time.

Examples of Widely Varying Study Techniques Used by Adult Students

Adults often find their own highly individual study methods to be most effective. Here are some vivid examples of diverse study methods used by adult students to earn their college degrees.

One Californian was versed in meditation techniques. In studying a textbook, he would use those meditation techniques to give the reading his complete concentration and would stop whenever his attention wandered. Then he would gradually "center" his attention and resume study in an almost trancelike state.

An older woman adopted very clear-cut methods for marking her textbooks. Other people, she noticed, seemed to underline almost every other sentence. Instead, she did the following:

- marked a big bracket beside the main idea
- traced a heavy double line under the most important term and a single line under the definition of that term

- wrote bold crosses in the margin next to particularly important points
- reread and analyzed any unclear sentences until she understood them clearly before going on
- summed up main points to remember by saying them out loud from time to time
- took notes on her reading in list or outline form on separate notebook sheets

In contrast, a retired army officer getting his degree picked out the key sentence in each paragraph and underlined only that. He would quickly check through all the key sentences in ending the assignment to fix the major points in memory. Later, to prepare for final examinations, he would make sure he understood all the underlined key sentences.

Another man worked as a salesperson and spent much time driving to call on customers. He found a tape recorder very helpful to use in his studies. While reading a textbook, he would make a study tape by recording a few sentences from each section or chapter, and especially include key terms and definitions. He could summarize large amounts of reading in a 30-minute recording. Then, while he was driving or even when getting dressed in the morning, he could study effectively by listening to the tapes.

Books to Consult on Improving Your Study Skills

Books entirely devoted to study skills that may be helpful to you include the following. These and similar books are available in public libraries and in bookstores.

James Deese and Ellin K. Deese, *How to Study: Morgan and Deese's Classic Handbook for Students,* 3d ed. New York: McGraw-Hill, 1979.

Gene R. Hawes and Lynn Salop Hawes, *Hawes Guide to Successful Study Skills: How to Earn High Marks in Your Courses and Tests.* New York: New American Library, 1981.

Eric Jensen, *You Can Succeed: The Ultimate Learning Guide for Students.* Woodbury, N.Y.: Barron's, 1979.

David Marshak, *HM Study Skills Program: Teacher's Guide, Student Text, Level III for College Freshmen.* Reston, Va.: National Association of Secondary School Principals, 1980.

Sheila Tobias, *Overcoming Math Anxiety.* New York: Norton, 1978.

10. Managing Time

Finding the time needed for study poses one of the main challenges for working adults enrolled in college, but millions of them do meet this challenge today. Here are suggestions for using proven time mangement techniques to solve your problems in finding enough time.

Make and Maintain a Weekly Pattern
of Time Allocation

Most adult students find it essential to follow a weekly schedule for allocating their time. Their work and home responsibilities run in weekly patterns. Once they have incorporated their weekly class sessions into those patterns, they also establish a pattern of regular hours for study.

One good way to help you maintain a pattern of study hours is to make a written schedule. You can use a standard desk calendar or pocket calendar for such written schedules, or you can use a one-week study-schedule form like that shown in Worksheet 9. A sample schedule has been filled in with a typical pattern of hours for an adult student, Hugh Barnes. You can photocopy the blank form for your own use.

Let's take a detailed look at Hugh's weekly schedule to determine his approach to allocating study time. His total of eight class hours per week is

WORKSHEET 9. STUDY HOURS SCHEDULE—
WEEK OF:

Day of Week	Class Time	Planned Study Hours	Actual Study Hours
Monday	_____	_____	_____
	_____	_____	_____
		_____	_____
Tuesday	_____	_____	_____
	_____	_____	_____
		_____	_____
Wednesday	_____	_____	_____
	_____	_____	_____
		_____	_____
Thursday	_____	_____	_____
	_____	_____	_____
		_____	_____
Friday	_____	_____	_____
	_____	_____	_____
		_____	_____
Saturday	_____	_____	_____
	_____	_____	_____
		_____	_____
Sunday	_____	_____	_____
	_____	_____	_____
		_____	_____

For: Hugh Barnes

STUDY HOURS SCHEDULE—WEEK OF: __12/9__

Day of Week	Class Time	Planned Study Hours	Actual Study Hours
Monday	7–8 p.m.	6–7 a.m.	
		6:30–7 p.m.	
		9–10 p.m.	
Tuesday		6–7 a.m.	
		8:30–10 p.m.	
Wednesday	7–10 p.m.	6–7 a.m.	
		6:30–7 p.m.	
Thursday		6–7 a.m.	
		8:30–10 p.m.	
Friday	7–8 p.m.	6–7 a.m.	
		6:30–7 p.m.	
Saturday	9 a.m.–noon	3–5 p.m.	
Sunday		8–10 a.m.	
		3:30–5 p.m.	
	(or)	7:30–9 p.m.	

a moderately heavy part-time schedule. He has to put in at least two hours of outside study for every one hour in class. Following that ratio, Hugh schedules a total of sixteen hours of study a week.

Because he has a wife and two small children, Hugh plans his schedule around his family life as well as the full-time job to which he commutes. A "morning person," he awakes before the family to put in a quiet hour of study every weekday before breakfasting and leaving for work.

On his Monday, Wednesday, and Friday class nights, Hugh goes directly from work to the college and has a sandwich in the student cafeteria to hold him until his late dinner at home. He spends a half hour each of those nights in the college library studying just before class. On Monday night he puts in another hour of study when he gets home.

Tuesday and Thursday nights he puts off studying until he's spent some time with the family and it's almost the children's bedtime. In fact, Daddy's study time is a period when the children start quieting down for the night.

Friday night after class he leaves open to spend with his wife. They sometimes have his mother baby-sit while they go out and do something like visiting friends or going to a movie or lecture or student dance at the college.

Hugh skips his 6 o'clock study session Saturday mornings, since he spends all Saturday morning at college pursuing his partial weekend college program. He schedules two study hours Saturday afternoon and leaves Saturday night and sometimes Sunday night open to spend with the family or to help with home chores. Sunday morning he puts in a quiet two hours of study and another hour and a half on Sunday afternoon or evening.

He varies the schedule as needed, for family occasions and problems on the one hand and for extra college tasks like term papers or exams on the other. He makes such shifts by adding and moving time blocks on his schedule chart. Hugh also keeps a record on the chart of the hours he actually spends studying in order to see if any adjustments in the plan are called for.

Study Schedule Rules to Follow

Generally helpful rules for you to consider in planning and carrying out your study schedule are as follows. (You've already seen some of the rules applied in the Hugh Barnes schedule.)

1. *Schedule at least two hours of study for every hour of class time.* As mentioned earlier, colleges typically advise students to study a minimum of two hours for every one hour spent in class. Some college departments with heavy academic demands advise three or four hours of outside study.

In your own case, schedule time according to your professors' advice and the demands of your courses, starting with two hours for every one hour of class time and increasing or decreasing as needed.

2. *Limit regular study periods to two hours or less, with several short breaks.* It's wiser to plan for a number of moderate-length study sessions through the week than for one or two very long days of study on the weekend. Your mind tends to stay more alert during shorter sessions of two hours or less, and what you learn seems to sink in better with short sessions.

Take 5-minute breaks from studying every 45 or 60 minutes. Stand up, stretch, look out the window, get a glass of water or a cup of coffee. After your break you'll work more effectively, with better concentration.

3. *Schedule study sessions just before or after class.* If you can, schedule even a short study period just before or after a class session. Doing so gives you the advantage of having your previous assignment or the latest classwork fresh in your mind for better learning in or following class.

4. *Use rewards to reinforce your motivation.* Give yourself little rewards during study breaks and just after your study periods. Juice, tea, or coffee could represent rewards for a break. Rewards following a study session might be a phone call to a friend, a stroll outdoors, or a half hour of jogging, reading a magazine or novel, or watching TV.

Such rewards can bolster your motivation for studying and serve as the "positive reinforcement" recommended by psychologists who specialize in learning theory and experiments. Without rewards, motivation to study can in large part be negative—fear of low marks, disapproval, or embarrassment. It's more productive to rely on positive motivation whenever you can.

Still other positive reinforcements develop as you start making progress in your studies. Gaining new knowledge and powers can prove richly rewarding in itself once you find you can do it successfully.

11. Using College Services and Asserting Your Student Rights

Should you need additional help with your studies or with problems surrounding them, look into student services offered by your college. Colleges often provide extensive services today to help students resolve various problems and get the most out of college.

Moreover, for problems that may arise between students and their professors or administrators, students have a number of rights. Knowing what these rights are and how to assert them can be important to your success in college.

Support Services for Help with Problems

How wide a range of student services on which you might draw is suggested by the typical provisions of representative colleges.

For help with studies, as an example, Amarillo College in Texas (a public two-year college) operates a Learning Resources Center in its five-story library building. There you can get help with reading and study skills from the ACcess Center office and from the English Writing Laboratory. Peer tutors are available free in almost any subject through the ACcess Tutoring and Study Skills Lab.

You can obtain not only books to help with your learning but also audiotapes, videotapes, and computer-augmented programs. The facilities include typewriters, copy machines, calculators, audio- and videocasette players, and even a biorhythm calculator.

Should personal problems or academic quandaries be interfering with your studies at Amarillo, you can turn to the Counseling Center, where professional counselors offer help with the following:

- severe personal or social troubles hampering your adjustment to college
- career exploration and planning, with aid from a Guidance Information System computer program and possible referral to the college's Career Center
- testing of interests and abilities for career and educational guidance, with related counseling
- General Educational Development (GED) tests for students who need high school equivalency diplomas
- program planning and course advisement to help you decide on a major

The Office of Women's Programs at Amarillo provides services for its large numbers of returning women students. Women constitute some 57 percent of the college's enrollment, and many are over age 24. Services provided for the returning woman student include

- referral help concerning family, legal, medical, child-care, and housing needs
- orientation sessions for the older-than-average student
- personal, educational, and career guidance
- job-market information and placement help
- financial aid information

At another college, the University of Wisconsin—Milwaukee (UWM), you can get medical and psychological help from the Norris Health Center. It is staffed by physicians, dentists, psychologists, certified athletic trainers, nurses, and medical technologists. It provides counseling and psychotherapy on an individual or a group basis. Most of its services are offered at no charge to enrolled students.

As with many colleges today, UWM offers extensive services for disabled students. These services make it possible for students with almost any physical handicap to enroll in and complete degree programs. Information about the services is available in the *UWM Handbook for Handicapped Students*.

You can pursue intramural, club, and recreational sports as a UWM student through the Klotsche Center for Physical Education. Social and cultural activities are available through the UWM Union, which provides student lounges, restaurants, a full schedule of mixers, dances, and other social functions, and even movie theaters and an art gallery.

Children of students are looked after at the UWM Day-Care Center. The center cares for children ranging in age from six months to five years (or up to age ten during summer sessions). It is professionally administered and staffed through the UWM School of Education.

Services vary among colleges, of course. But these two are typical examples, not exceptions, that illustrate what you should be able to expect from your college.

Student Rights

Your rights as a college student are (1) official and (2) customary or traditional. Knowing what your rights are can help you if some difficulty or dispute arises with a college office or professor.

Official rights are usually summed up in the college's catalog or a separate handbook. Official academic regulations also often include general policies regarding student rights.

Many important rights concerning the student's official college records stem from the 1975 Family Educational Rights and Privacy Act (a federal statute, Public Law 93-380). Your major rights under this law include (1) your rights to privacy of those records, providing in essence that they cannot be made accessible to third parties outside the institution without your consent, or even to officers of the institution without legitimate needs to use the records in your interest; and (2) your rights to have access to those records and to challenge the content of those records as untrue, if justified.

Other official rights due you under federal and state laws include the right to be treated with no discrimination whatever on the grounds of your race, sex, age, or ethnic heritage.

Student rights that are more often semiofficial, procedural, or customary include the following:

- Grade appeal. This right permits you to submit a dispute over a test or course grade to an arbitrator, such as the department head or a special student-faculty grievance committee.
- Adjustment of course requirements for illness or personal emergencies. This right permits you to make up missed examinations, to have extensions of due dates for papers or research projects, or to substitute independent study for classwork missed because of unavoidable absences.
- Proper and professional conduct of instruction in a course. This right

permits you, in the unlikely event your instructor is unqualified· or unprofessional, to appeal to the department head or academic dean.

Right to Grade Appeal

The following practices concerning the right of grade appeal are used at Hunter College of the City University of New York. Suppose that you believed your final grade of C came far below the A-minus or A you figured you deserved on the basis of marks on your exams and papers and your classroom participation.

You would first see the course instructor or the department secretary to find out if a clerical error had been made. If not, you would then confer with the instructor. Should the instructor make no change and should you still disagree with the grade, you would submit an appeal in writing to the department chairperson, basing your appeal on facts.

In response, the chairperson would notify the instructor and appoint a department review committee for which you could request that one member be a student. Then, if you or the instructor disagreed with the committee's finding, either might make an appeal to the Standing Committee on Grade Appeals of the Hunter College Senate. Its membership consists of four faculty members and three students. After review, its decision is final.

Right to Freedom from Sexual Harassment

Sexual harassment of women students and even of women faculty members at colleges has come increasingly to light in recent years. As a result, the right to protection from such harassment has become widely established among colleges. The right to such protection is based not just on college practices and policies but on federal and state laws concerning civil rights and discrimination. If you should happen to experience sexual harassment in pursuing your college studies, submit a written report at once to the dean.

If any further incidents or reprisals develop, send a copy of your report— expanded to include such incidents or reprisals, along with the names of any witnesses—to the state attorney general and to the office of the United States attorney for the district of the federal court system serving the college's locale. You're not likely to have to take such action, but you should know that it's available to you.

Accommodations Above and Beyond Rights

Although colleges are bureaucratic of necessity, many professors and administrators are willing to go far out of their way to help serious and ambitious students. If you need some special adaptation of the rules for convincing reasons, ask for them.

For instance, ask for permission to get into a closed course if not being able to take that course will seriously interfere with your program. Request an extension on a due date for a term paper if family illness makes it impossible to have the paper done on time. See if you can raise your final grade in a course by doing a special research paper or other substantial additional work beyond regular assignments. If you've been conscientious and hard-working all along, you're likely to have such requests granted.

By and large, colleges want to help you succeed. In all probability, you'll be able to count on your college's goodwill in fulfilling its mission of helping you develop your capabilities to the fullest.

Glossary
of College Terms

Given here are generally accepted definitions of college terms with which students should be familiar. The individual college, however, may define a term differently, and students should consult the catalogs and bulletins of specific institutions for descriptions of their programs and procedures.

Academic year. The aggregate of annual study terms of a college or university, usually extending from the opening of classes each August or September through final examinations and graduation in the spring. Commonly, the academic year of an American college consists of two semesters or three quarters, followed by an additional summer session (with possible short intersessions) of course offerings.

Accreditation. Approval by a recognized accrediting organization of a college or university, or a study program, for meeting specified minimum standards of quality in its instruction, staffing, facilities, financial stability, and policies. Regional accreditation applies to the college or university as a whole and is granted by one of six regional associations of colleges and secondary schools in the United States. Professional accreditation applies to the study program or programs in a specific career field or academic subject and is typically granted by a major national professional or academic society in that field or discipline. State accreditation or approval of a college usually represents a minimum level of quality assurance and is required for a college or university to offer instruction to the public.

Achievement Tests. College Board tests in specific college preparatory subjects. Required by some colleges for admission and used also in course placement.

American College Testing Program Assessment (ACT). The test battery of the American College Testing Program. Required for admission by many colleges and universities.

Application for Federal Student Aid. A form that may be used by students applying for federally sponsored financial aid for college students, chiefly Pell Grants and Guaranteed Student Loans.

Associate degree. The degree granted by a college or university for completion of a study program normally taking two years of full-time study (or longer, in part-time study).

Career services office or **center.** A college office or department providing services to assist students in choosing careers, in developing skills in searching and qualifying for jobs, and in actually finding and obtaining jobs. The office provides listings of job openings and interviews with corporate and government recruiters visiting the campus. Such an office might also be identified as a placement bureau, student placement office, or career resources center.

Challenge examinations. Examinations offered by a college that are prepared in specific subjects by its own faculty members and that enable students to earn credits by passing the examinations instead of attending class sessions.

College Board. An education association whose members include colleges and secondary schools. It provides college entrance examinations (including the Scholastic Aptitude Test and Achievement Tests) and has as a constituent association the College Scholarship Service. Many testing and scholarship services of the Board are administered by Educational Testing Service (ETS), a nonprofit education organization.

College-Level Examination Program (CLEP). A College Board program of examinations in undergraduate college subjects. Widely used by colleges to award degree credit to students for nontraditional college-level learning. See credit by examination.

College Scholarship Service (CSS). A constituent association of the College Board offering services designed to provide for the equitable distribution of financial aid funds for college students by determining each student's financial need. Its Financial Aid Form (FAF) is used to obtain family financial information from applicants for aid.

College Work-Study Program (CWSP). A federally sponsored financial aid program that provides jobs for students with demonstrated financial need.

Contract learning program. A college study program in which the student studies independently and at periodic intervals (such as every few months) makes a learning agreement or contract with a faculty adviser, which defines the learning to be carried out during the term of that agreement or contract.

Cooperative work-study program. A study program offered by more than 900 colleges in which the student alternates between periods of full-time study and full-time employment in a field related to the study area, as in engineering or business administration.

Correspondence study course. A course (which can be one recognized for degree credit and conducted by a regionally accredited college) for which the student registers and receives and sends course materials by mail, and in which the student learns independently without class attendance (usually proceeding on a lesson-by-lesson basis with lesson assignments guided, graded, and returned by a teacher assigned to the student for the course).

Credit. Unit widely used by colleges to specify amounts of study that a student must complete with satisfactory performance in order to qualify for an academic degree. Generally, a course meeting one hour a week through a semester carries one semester-hour credit, a course meeting two hours a week carries two semester-hour credits, and so on. A total of at least 120 credits is required for a bachelor's degree, and at least 60 credits are required for an associate degree. Colleges operating on a quarter calendar use a similar system based on quarter-hour credits, with 3 quarter-hour credits usually equivalent to 2 semester-hour credits.

Credit by examination. Credit toward a degree awarded by a college on the basis of a student's performance on specified examinations (such as a college's own challenge examinations or those of the College-Level Examination Program).

Educational Testing Service (ETS). See College Board.

Elective course. A course that a student takes by choice as distinguished from a course specifically required for a degree.

Equivalency diploma. A diploma officially recognized as a certificate of high school graduation. Earned by passing specified examinations, usually the General Educational Development (GED) tests, rather than through customary high school attendance.

Experiential learning credit. Degree credit awarded by a college through procedures it specifies for evaluating the kind and amount of college-level learning acquired by a student in previous experience at work or in other activities; also called life experience credit.

External degree program. A study program or set of study programs offered by a college in which a student can earn a degree with little or no attendance at the college (often, through some combination of credit by examination, transfer credit, experiential learning credit, independent study, and credit for prior coursework outside colleges).

Family Financial Statement (FFS). The financial information collection form used by the Financial Aid Services office of the American College Testing Program in determining a student's financial need. See financial need.

Financial Aid Form (FAF). The financial information collection form used by the College Scholarship Service in determining a student's financial need. See financial need.

Financial need. The difference between what the student and her/his spouse (or parents) can afford to spend toward that student's college costs and the total of those costs, as computed in the need analysis systems used by colleges and other aid sponsors. In those systems, colleges and other sponsors require aid applicants to complete family financial information collection forms to provide basic data for the computations.

4-1-4 academic year calendar. A variant of the two-semester academic year calendar in which the academic year consists of a four-month fall semester, a one-month winter intersession, and a four-month spring semester.

Full-time study. The enrollment status of a student who is registered for at least 12 semester-hour credits (or at least 12 quarter-hour credits) per term of the regular academic year, as usually defined by colleges; part-time study is the enrollment status of students registered for fewer credits per term than the minimum set by the college for full-time study.

General Educational Development (GED) tests. A series of five tests that adults who did not complete high school may take to qualify for an equivalency diploma.

Grade point average (GPA). A numerical index of overall student academic performance. It is calculated by first multiplying the number of credits earned in each completed course by the numerical value of the student's grade in that course (generally $A = 4$, $B = 3$, $C = 2$, $D = 1$, and E or $F = 0$). All the resulting grade points for each course are then added, and their sum is divided by the total number of credits taken. (A student who has earned A grades in all courses will have a GPA of 4.0, for example.) For high school GPAs, the number of class hours or periods per week for each course is used instead of the number of credits earned for the course.

Graduate study program, graduate degree. A study program for which a bachelor's degree or the equivalent is usually required for admission; a degree earned through a graduate study program.

Guaranteed Student Loan (GSL) Program. A federally sponsored program of financial aid in which students may take out loans for college costs at subsidized interest rates, and for which financial need is an eligibility requirement.

Independent study. A program that does not require class attendance for degree credit. The student learns independently under the supervision of a faculty member.

Life experience credit. See experiential learning credit.

Major. The subject or career field that serves as the area of concentration in the student's study program for a degree. For a bachelor's degree, students must commonly earn about one-fourth of their credits in the major.

National Direct Student Loan (NDSL) Program. A federally sponsored program of financial aid in which students may take out loans for college costs at subsidized interest rates (rates lower than those in the GSL program), and for which financial need is an eligibility requirement.

Ombudsperson. The administrative officer at some colleges whose major duties are to receive and rectify grievances reported by students.

Part-time study. See full-time study.

Pell Grant Program. A federally sponsored program of financial aid in which college students may qualify for grants adjusted in amount according to financial need.

Placement office. See career services office.

Proficiency Examination Program (PEP). A program of examinations in undergraduate college subjects widely used by colleges to award degree credit to students by examination, and offered by the American College Testing Program. See credit by examination.

Quarter. See academic year.

Registration. (1) For a college academic term, the process by which the student chooses, enrolls in, and pays for course sessions for the term; also, the period of several days before the term opening designated by the college for carrying out that process. (2) For entrance tests required by a college for admission, the process by which the student chooses and enrolls for (and pays for) the test date and test center location at which to take the test or tests.

Requirements. (1) For a college degree, the amounts and kinds of study stipulated by the college as necessary in order to qualify for that degree. (2) For college admission, the documents, test results, and possibly minimum qualifications and interview, stipulated by the college as necessary in order to qualify for admission.

Scholastic Aptitude Test (SAT). A test of verbal and mathematical reasoning abilities that is required for admission by many colleges and universities and is offered by the College Board.

Supplemental Educational Opportunity Grant (SEOG) Program. A federally sponsored program of financial aid providing grant assistance and administered by colleges, and for which high-need students may qualify automatically if they have applied for both federal and college aid.

Terminal study program. A study program usually offered by a two-year community college that is designed to qualify students for immediate employment upon completing the program rather than for transfer to a bachelor's degree program; many terminal programs lead to an associate degree.

Transcript. An official record of the courses taken and grades earned by a student throughout high school or in one or more colleges.

Transfer credit. Credit accepted by a college toward a degree on the basis of prior study by the student at another college.

Transfer program. A study program usually offered by a two-year community college that is designed to qualify students completing the program for transfer to a bachelor's degree program with little or no loss of credit; most transfer programs lead to an associate degree.

Trimester. An alternate name for semester employed by colleges that offer year-round study. Three trimesters make up one year (with the third trimester representing their summer sessions).

Undergraduate. Pertaining to studies for associate or bachelor's degrees.

Upper-division. Pertaining to studies on the level of the junior and senior years of study for a bachelor's degree (the last two years of study for a bachelor's, in conventional full-time study programs).

Weekend college study program. A study program designed especially for working adults in which students attend course sessions primarily or entirely during weekends; in many such programs, the student may be able to earn a degree in as few years as students in conventional full-time programs leading to that degree.

Work-study. (1) See cooperative work-study program. (2) See College Work-Study Program.

Bibliography

Career and Education Planning

Crystal, John C., and Richard Bolles. *Where Do I Go from Here with My Life?: A Very Systematic, Practical, and Effective Life/Work Planning Manual for Students, Counselors, Career Seekers, and Career Changers.* Berkeley, Calif.: Ten Speed Press, 1974.

Holland, John L. *The Self-Directed Search: A Guide to Educational and Vocational Planning.* Palo Alto, Calif.: Consulting Psychologists Press, 1970. Presents an occupational interests inventory you can administer and score yourself, with keys and explanations enabling you to use your inventory results to find career fields likely to fit your interests.

Regents Degree Program: A Self-Assessment and Self-Planning Manual (by Linda Headley Walker, et. al.). Albany: University of the State of New York Regents Degree Program, 1983. The book's long Career Exploration section guides the reader through self-assessment, choosing careers and planning education accordingly, and effective job searching. Available for $5 a copy, payable to University of the State of New York, from Regents Degree Program, Cultural Education Center, Room 5D45, Albany, NY 12230.

Facts about Career Fields

Hawes, Gene R. *Encyclopedia of Second Careers.* New York: Facts on File, 1984. Extensive reference work found in a number of libraries.

Mitchell, Joyce Slayton. *I Can Be Anything: A Career Book for Women*, 3d ed. New York: College Entrance Examination Board, 1982.

Mitchell, Joyce Slayton. *Choices and Changes: A Career Book for Men*. New York: College Entrance Examination Board, 1982.

U.S. Department of Labor. *Occupational Outlook Handbook*. Washington, D.C.: U.S. Government Printing Office. Issued biannually and widely available in libraries.

U.S. Department of Labor. *Occupational Outlook Quarterly*. Washington, D.C.: U.S. Government Printing Office. Helpful for reports on current trends in career fields and for facts on selected careers. Widely available in libraries.

Colleges, Study Programs, and Accreditation

American Council on Education. *Accredited Institutions of Postsecondary Education*, Sherry S. Harris, ed. Washington, D.C.: American Council on Education. Revised annually. (Distributed by Macmillan, New York.) Widely available in libraries, this work is the central reference source on the regional accreditation status of colleges and universities and on the professional accreditation status of degree-credit programs in individual career fields.

American Council on Education. *Guide to External Degree Programs in the United States*, Eugene Sullivan, ed., Washington, D.C.: American Council on Education. Revised every few years. A directory of external degree programs offered by colleges and universities, in which students can earn degrees on flexible schedules and with little or no class attendance.

College Board. *The College Handbook*, New York: College Entrance Examination Board. Revised annually. (Distributed by Scribners, New York.) An extensive, annually revised general directory of American colleges and universities and their undergraduate programs.

National Commission for Cooperative Education. *Undergraduate Programs of Cooperative Education in the United States and Canada*, Cooperative Education Research Center of Northeastern University, ed., 11th ed. Boston: National Commission for Cooperative Education, 1984. Available on request to the commission at 360 Huntington Avenue, Boston, MA 02115. Identifies the cooperative work-study programs offered by more than 900 colleges and universities and gives summary facts about them.

National University Continuing Education Association. *The Independent Study Catalog*, Peterson's Guides, ed. Princeton, N.J.: Peterson's Guides. Revised annually. An extensive directory of degree-credit correspondence courses offered by regionally accredited colleges.

Simosko, Susan. *Earn College Credit for What You Know.* Washington, D.C.:
    Acropolis Books, 1984. Identifies more than 500 colleges that grant
    degree credit for experiential learning, and explains how to qualify for
    such credit.

Financial Aid

American Federation of Labor-Congress of Industrial Organizations. *AFL-
    CIO Guide to Union-Sponsored Scholarships, Awards and Student Finan-
    cial Aid 1985,* AFL-CIO Department of Education, ed. Washington,
    D.C.: AFL-CIO. Revised annually. Single copies of 1985 edition free
    to members, $3 to others; available from AFL-CIO Department of
    Education, 815 16th Street NW, Washington, DC 20006. A directory
    of union-sponsored scholarships that are often offered for members as
    well as for children of members.
O'Neill, Joseph P. *Corporate Tuition Aid Programs: A Directory of College
    Financial Aid for Employees at America's Largest Corporations.* Princeton,
    NJ: Conference University Press, 1984. Reports on replies from 650
    companies employing more than 17 million Americans, based on a
    survey of the industrial "Fortune 500" and service "Fortune 500"
    companies.
U.S. Department of Education. *The Student Guide: Five Federal Financial
    Aid Programs;* and *Application for Federal Student Aid.* Washington,
    D.C.: U.S. Government Printing Office. Revised annually. Available
    free on request from Federal Student Aid Programs, Department DEA-
    086, Pueblo, CO 81009.

Index

Planning for adult college attendance (continued)
   career and income goals, achieving by, 8
   what programs for which careers, 10
Possible promotions at work as result of college study, 102
Prior learning, credits granted for, 36–37
   Earn Credit For What You Know, 37
Professors and instructors
   help offered by, 100
   relating to, 100
   discussions with, effect of, 100
Professionally accredited college programs, locating, 27
Professional societies, scholarships available through, 85

Quarter system
   calendars, use of, 34

Range of student services and facilities, 117–120
Reading required
   intensive reading, skills required, 105–107
   preliminary survey, effect, 105, 107
   speed and comprehension, boosting, 105–106
Recreational life of student
   adjustments necessary following start of course, 103–104
Registration
   activities at, 95
   advisers, need for in connection with, 95–96
   assistance at, need for, 95
      sources of, 96
   catalog listings, usefulness, 96
   coping with, 97
   counselors to advise at, need for, 95–96
   course selection and schedule, planning, 96
   fees and tuition, payment of, 97

installment payments, availability, 97
   student ID card, receipt of on payment, 97–98
   elements of the card, 97–98
   uses of, 98
   possible combinations, setting up, 96
   substitutions, planning, 97
   schedule and course selection, planning, 96
   student ID card
      receipt of, 97–98
      elements of, 97–98
      uses, 98
   tuition and fees, payment of, 97
      installment payments, availability, 97
      student ID card, receipt of on payment, 97–98
      elements of the card, 97–98
      uses of the card, 98
Relating to other students, effect, 100
Relating to professors and instructors, 100
Requirements for degee completion, 33–34

Scholastic Aptitude Test (SAT), required use of in admissions, 92–93
Securing financial aid
   See also. Financial aid
   procedures, 86–87, 90
   forms for, use, 90
Self-supporting students, criteria as to financial need, 80
Services provided by the college
   children of students, day care centers for, 119
   disabled students, for, 118
   facilities available, 117–118
   General Educational Development (GED) tests, availability, 118
   personal problems, help with, 118
   problems, support services for helping with, 117–119
   range of, 117–119